ANGRY MEN AND THE WOMEN WHO LOVE THEM

*Breaking the
Cycle of
Physical and
Emotional Abuse*

PAUL HEGSTROM

*A short-tempered man must bear his own penalty;
you can't do much to help him. If you try
you must try a dozen times!* (Prov. 19:19, TLB)

BEACON HILL PRESS
OF KANSAS CITY

ISBN 978-0-8341-2152-2

Printed in the
United States of America

Cover Design: Ted Ferguson

All Scripture quotations not otherwise designated are from the *Holy Bible, New International Version*® (NIV®). Copyright © 1973, 1978, 1984 by International Bible Society. Used by permission of Zondervan Publishing House. All rights reserved.

Permission to quote from the following additional copyrighted versions of the Bible is acknowledged with appreciation:

The *Amplified Bible* (AMP.). The *Amplified New Testament* (AMP.), copyright © 1954, 1958, 1987 by The Lockman Foundation.

The *New Revised Standard Version* (NRSV) of the Bible, copyright 1989 by the Division of Christian Education of the National Council of the Churches of Christ in the USA. All rights reserved.

The Living Bible (TLB), © 1971. Used by permission of Tyndale House Publishers, Inc., Wheaton, IL 60189. All rights reserved.

Scripture quotations marked KJV are from the King James Version.

Library of Congress Cataloging-in-Publication Data

Hegstrom, Paul, 1941-
    Angry men and the women who love them : breaking the cycle of physical and emotional abuse/ Paul Hegstrom. — Rev. ed.
        p. cm.
    Includes bibliographical references (p.   ).
    ISBN 0-8341-2152-2 (pbk.)
    1. Family violence—United States. 2. Wife abuse—United States. 3. Abusive men—United States—Psychology. 4. Family violence—Religious aspects—Christianity. 5. Wife abuse—Religious aspects—Christianity. I. Title.

    HV6626.2.H44 2004
    616. 85'822—dc22

                                                                    2004011207

10   9   8   7

To my six grandchildren, who because of my crisis and subsequent willingness to break the cycle of violence live in peaceful homes free of emotional and physical abuse.

CONTENTS

ACKNOWLEDGMENTS

There are many people I want to acknowledge and thank for their encouragement and support in this project. Writing this book has been a humbling experience as I have purposely gone back to my painful past and the beginning of my recovery—reliving it step-by-step.

My wife, Judy, has been a support during the research, adaptations, and application of these skills in my life, as have been my children: Tammy, Heidi, and Jeff.

I express my gratitude to Lenore Walker, whose pioneering work in the field of domestic violence was all I had in the late 1970s, when my own need was so great. Others who influenced my research and my life read like a "who's who" in the field, including the Domestic Abuse Project in Minneapolis.

A special thanks to Mary Rebar of the State's Attorney Office in Champaign County, Illinois, for her wise input as we structured this book, and for her knowledge of court systems and victims' services.

I cannot leave out my pastor, Tim Stearman, who took a chance on me when others were doubting my recovery, and Keith Showalter, who vouched for me. Pastor Tim, you are the finest pastor I have ever sat under.

Beacon Hill Press of Kansas City, you have been patient with me in the writing and editing of this book. Thank you from the bottom of my heart.

To all involved, thank you.

Chapter 1

THE BACKGROUND

PAUL'S STORY

When I was nine years old I accepted God's call to ministry. Six months later, I was sexually molested. I remember feeling dirty, damaged, and different. Surely Jesus could never use a "dirty" little boy like me to further His kingdom.

I tried to talk to my parents about what had happened to me, but in those days, "nice" people didn't talk about such things. I was reprimanded for even using the word *sex*.

Several weeks after my first attempt to discuss my molestation with my parents, I asked my mother a hypothetical question: "If my friend David was molested by an old man, what would happen to him?"

"Why, you would never be allowed to play with David again!" she replied.

"Why?"

"Because David would be ruined, he'd be damaged, and he'd know about things that children shouldn't know about. You just could never play with him again."

When I think back to my life as a child, I remember how I enjoyed my calm Christian home. My dad was a preacher, and although he was a great communicator in the pulpit, the one sad spot in my life at that time was that he didn't really know how to communicate with his family. Every morning as he left the house, he simply shook my hand. I wanted desperately for him to scoop me up in his arms for a big hug.

One of the privileges of being a preacher's kid was getting to meet the missionaries who came to our church. One of my favorites was Louise Chapman. She served in Africa for many years, and she told stories of witch doctors and black mamba snakes. She shared how God had spared her life in many situations.

One night I asked her what it felt like when God calls you to ministry.

She explained in terms that a nine-year-old boy could understand, and tears filled my eyes. "That's just what's been happening to me!" I exclaimed to her. "I'm willing to do anything Jesus wants me to do."

Mrs. Chapman put her hands on my forehead and prayed for me. I was so excited that God had chosen me to serve Him.

So when I was not allowed to deal with the truth of my molestation when it occurred, and since I was well aware of the "mark" that was on me through my hypothetical question about my friend David, I successfully banished that experience to my subconscious. For the next 31 years I had no memory of it.

I met my future wife, Judy, when my family moved to her hometown. She was 13, and I was 15. By the time we began dating, I had developed a Jekyll-and-Hyde personality—no doubt due to my early sexual awareness that resulted from being molested. I was considered exciting, funny, the town clown—but I had no interpersonal skills because my emotional development had been arrested at a tender age.

As we dated, I began to be abusive toward Judy. Because of my arrested development, I felt like a little boy with an older, good-looking girl who someone might try to steal away from me. Subconsciously I set out to destroy her self-esteem so that she wouldn't dare leave me for someone else.

We married when I was 19 and Judy was 17—primarily because I needed to possess her. We were planning to elope, but when her mother discovered our plans, she said to me, "If we stop you now, you'll just try again. Call your father and tell him to come perform the ceremony."

We got married on Saturday, and by Sunday I was abusing Judy both physically and emotionally. It was the beginning of a miserable existence that lasted for 16 years.

I hated what I was. But I thought that maybe going into

the ministry would help me overcome my bad behavior. Not really a good reason for entering ministry.

Judy and I pastored a small church in Iowa. Even though I was a broken vessel myself, the church grew and people got saved. What a testament to the Word of God!

I had been able to stop my abusive behavior during the first six weeks of our pastorate. But since it was a small church, I had to work out of town to earn a living, and the stress began to take its toll. Eventually I developed a pattern of fighting with Judy when I arrived home. I knocked holes in the walls of the parsonage and battered Judy and our children. Sometimes she locked herself in the bathroom, but I could break right through the doorjamb. She had no safe place.

For three years we lived this kind of existence. I had no control over my life and was powerless to change. I knew I was wrong, and repeatedly I knelt at the altar and cried, *God, why can't I change? Why am I so driven in this relationship? Why am I like this?*

Since no answers were forthcoming, I developed the approach of, *Well, God, You called me to the ministry. If You will help Judy straighten up, I'll be OK.* I actually asked God to hit her in the head with a two-by-four to get her attention and make her obedient and submissive so I wouldn't behave so badly. I blamed her for my problem.

Finally I couldn't take the pressure of living a lie while I was trying to pastor, and I deserted the church and my family. My solution was to turn my back on God and everything I had believed.

Judy and I were separated for 3½ years and then divorced. During the following three years I lived with another woman in a relationship that was even more violent than my marriage to Judy. I hurt that woman so badly that she fled to a shelter and called the police. There, she learned her rights and what the results would be if she reported me to the police. I learned that what I had done could get me charged with attempted murder and that I could end up in prison for 15 to 22 years. She delivered an ultimatum: "Either get help by checking into a program and having an intake done in the next 12 hours or I'll give the police your name and address." She gave me the name of the program I was to attend and the name of the man I was to see.

My actions put me in jeopardy of an attempted murder charge that could have resulted in 15 to 22 years in prison.

That got my attention! I went into the mandated program and got private therapy. The program was a thumb in my back that motivated me to change.

Six months later, though, I was still telling the guys in my group that if it weren't for my ex-wife, if it weren't for my girlfriend, if it weren't for my parents, if it weren't for this, or if it weren't for that, things would be different. I was still in denial.

I remember so clearly when one of the other group members looked at me and said, "When are you gonna learn that it's not about them—it's about you?" This guy hadn't even accepted his own responsibilities yet, but he could see through me. That made me so angry that I decided I would not go back to group anymore—even if I had to face attempted murder charges.

Three nights later, though, in desperation I threw myself on the floor and pounded it. For two hours I screamed at God. *David was a man after Your own heart, yet he broke every commandment! You said You aren't a respecter of persons. I've pleaded with You! Why don't You hear me?*

I listed for God all the great men of the Bible and their sins. Then I said, *In James You said that if I ask for wisdom, You'll give it to me abundantly.*

After my rage I fell into self-pity. I cried until there were no more tears and my throat hurt. I had screamed at God for so long that I couldn't even whisper—my voice was gone. But in my heart, I heard, *The Father has heard your plea for wisdom, Paul. But you don't have a teachable spirit.*

I wondered, *But why? Why can I not stand authority? Why am I not teachable?*

Again, I felt a response. *If you will become teachable, the Father will give you a program that will restore your family. When it's done, He wants you to take it to a nation and eventually to a world.*

God, I don't even know how to be teachable. Will You show me?

God taught me that I needed to come to Him as a child. Then I needed to grow up. And I came to realize that I alone was responsible for my abusive behavior. I returned to the group and completed the program.

Some months later I called Judy. "Judy, there are some things happening in my life."

Initially she wanted nothing to do with me. But I was finally able to persuade her to meet with me, and we talked for hours. For the first time, we became friends. We dated for 11 months. God worked in our hearts and brought me to a new maturity as I began to grow up. He gave us a new love for each other—unlike our first relationship.

After seven years of separation and divorce, Judy and I remarried. That was in 1984, and since then there has not been a single incident of physical or emotional abuse.

Our kids came home for Christmas that first year and so enjoyed their time with us that our 23-year-old daughter said, "Dad, can I come home to live again?" I agreed.

After living at home a few months, she told her 22-year-old sister, "If Dad will let you, come home. This is a real trip!" Two hours later, on that recommendation, our younger daughter asked if she could come home too. Our son, Jeff, came home when he was 20, and we had the privilege of re-parenting our three adult children. They are all married now, of course, and Judy and I are grandparents.

Judy and I certainly had our share of difficulties, but out of those difficulties has come the program "Learning to Live, Learning to Love—Life Skills."

JUDY'S STORY

The first time I laid eyes on Paul Hegstrom was my first

year at teen camp. During a class on dating and marriage, the leader asked us to think about the traits we would like in our spouses. When we were asked to share our thoughts, the only one to speak out was Paul. He made some crass comment, and the boys laughed. We girls thought he was a jerk. Two months later, Paul moved to my hometown in Iowa and started attending my church.

Before long, Paul and I were an item in youth group. Our dating relationship was up and down, and I was constantly on edge. Nevertheless, when Paul insisted we get married while I was still a senior in high school, I agreed. My parents were against it, but they finally gave us their blessing, and we had a simple ceremony with just family members in attendance.

The day after our wedding was a Sunday—our first full day as man and wife. My brother was with us, and somehow he and Paul ended up in an argument. I tried to intervene, but Paul yelled, "This is none of your business!" He shoved me out of the room, and I fell. Suddenly I felt afraid of the person I had just married. Of course, he apologized. But he also added that it was really my own fault for interfering. And thus I began to accept blame for the abuse.

A few days later Paul criticized my intelligence.

"Too bad we all can't be as smart as you are," I retaliated.

Paul backhanded me in the face, breaking my glasses. As the blood poured, my brother simply watched. Later Paul offered to take me to the hospital, but I was afraid of him and asked him just to take me to my parents' house.

Paul dropped me off in the driveway so that he wouldn't have to face my dad. I begged Dad not to hurt Paul—and thus I began to lay the foundation for excusing Paul's behavior.

Paul and I moved four times in the first few months of our marriage—twice to other towns. I worked at hamburger stands, and that was the main reason I ever had anything to eat. Finally, one day I called my dad to tell him I was hungry and wanted to come home. I didn't really *want* to go home—I just wanted Paul to get a job and take care of me.

Not long after that I found out that I was pregnant, and

Paul and I moved to California. We would move continuously during our first years together. After our second daughter was born I remember asking Paul if we would ever settle down and have a home of our own. He angrily informed me that we would have to sacrifice so he could return to college.

He did pursue a degree in theology in Oklahoma around that time, but I became pregnant again, and he dropped out of school. He tried to be a family man, but his old ways returned. He spent money frivolously and didn't pay our utility bills or buy food with what little money we did have. Our neighbors ran an extension cord from their garage into our home so that I could care for our children after dark. Paul was not the slightest bit embarrassed that others were providing for his family; he was just glad he didn't have to be responsible for us.

Paul was called to a church in a small community, and I hoped our lives would change. As our children grew up, I tried to protect them from his behavior, but, of course, they were aware of what was going on.

It was humiliating that Paul was making good money but refused to take care of his family.

Instead of blaming Paul for his bad behavior, I blamed myself and tried to look perfect and perform perfectly. But nothing I did made him happy. The physical abuse continued to escalate. Once, while our children cried outside our locked bedroom door, Paul hit me so hard he knocked the wind out of me. The kids were screaming, asking if I was all right. I finally was able to tell them that I was fine, but they knew better. My children were not stupid—they were just helpless.

Eventually it became clear that Paul was seeing other women. He sometimes dressed up and left the house on holidays and Sundays to go see "clients." I found pornography, and he said it belonged to a friend who had hidden it in our house.

My children and I barely survived. Sometimes Paul would be gone for long periods of time, and we were desperate for food. Social Services would not provide food stamps because

Paul was earning money. A lady from our church was kind enough to bring us groceries. It was so humiliating that Paul was supposedly making good money but wouldn't take care of his family.

Paul continued to bounce in and out of our lives, but I was happiest when it was just me and the kids. Even when he lived away from us, though, he continued to control our lives. At one point our telephone was turned off because he hadn't paid the bill, but he still expected to talk to me every day and demanded that I go to a telephone two blocks away and wait for him to call.

We finally moved back together as a family, and as I was unpacking boxes, I opened one that I thought contained household items. I found in it a folded paper, and when I unfolded it, I read, "Hegstrom vs. Hegstrom." Unable to comprehend what I held in my hand, I called the attorney listed on the letterhead. He told me, "I'm sorry, Ma'am, but you're divorced."

The attorney explained that Paul had said he didn't know where I lived or how to contact me, so he had been awarded an uncontested divorce from me.

The children and I found a new apartment of our own and began to enjoy newfound freedom. I grappled spiritually with why God hadn't changed Paul and why I had suffered so in my relationship with Paul. Then one night the Lord spoke to me: *Don't pray for Paul to return. Pray for his soul.*

After weeks of praying for Paul and giving him to God, I realized I no longer had feelings for him. I was able to continue with my life alone. I began to see myself as a valuable person, capable of using my brain and acceptable to myself and others. The years passed smoothly.

When our younger daughter was ready to leave for college, I was afraid my car wouldn't make the 500-mile trip. I swallowed my pride and asked Paul if he would let me borrow his car to take her. He told me he and his girlfriend had broken up for good, although I didn't believe him and didn't really care. He said he didn't want me to drive that far alone and that he would take Heidi to school. I knew she wouldn't feel comfortable alone with him, so I said I would go along too.

On the drive home from taking her to college, Paul and I talked like normal human beings. There were no put-downs, no blaming. I wondered what in the world had happened to him. He told me he had been in therapy and that his attitudes were changing and that he was beginning to accept responsibility for his past behavior.

He started inviting me to meet him for coffee occasionally. We weren't dating—just talking. I left our talks feeling like a normal person. I could discuss things with him without him becoming angry. It didn't seem to affect him adversely when I didn't share his opinions on everything.

Eventually we were seeing each other regularly, but I was still cautious. One day he asked me if I had ever thought about getting back together. I told him I had thought about how different things might have been if he had been like this when we were married. I told him I could tell he had been working on himself and that I really liked the new guy. He seemed to be proud when I said that—but humble at the same time.

I asked God for direction. Soon I began having feelings of love for Paul that I had never felt during our marriage. Paul told me that he was having the same feelings, and that even though he was afraid, God had shown him that our family would be restored.

The weeks following our second wedding were wonderful. He was truly a changed man. The years of our second marriage have been happy ones. Although I've had to face some unresolved feelings and insecurities left over from our first marriage, I now live a happy, abuse-free existence with my husband.

Paul and I have learned so much, and it is our desire to share what the Lord has taught us on our journey. God provides help for us through the Bible and through His people. If you're an angry man, or a woman who loves an angry man, it is our prayer that you will benefit from our story.

Chapter 2

THE WIDE RANGE OF DOMESTIC VIOLENCE

Author and speaker Lonni Collins Pratt wrote the following about her experience with domestic violence:

What was I doing in a church again? After all, God and I weren't on speaking terms anymore.

Eight months ago, I curled up on the deck of a friend's boat and told God to go away. That was only weeks after receiving a diagnosis of leukemia and learning my husband had filed for divorce.

The divorce wasn't a surprise. My husband had demanded that I not be treated for my illness; he said people would talk if the pastor's wife went to doctors instead of God.

"If you would just trust God and pray!" he yelled at me as his fingers tightened around my throat. I knew there'd be bruises.

"If you would be an obedient wife, God would heal you," he continued as he slammed me against the bedroom wall. A dull pain shot through my neck to my shoulders. I shoved at him to get him away.

He grabbed my collar with both hands. I shut my eyes and prepared for what came next as he threw me against the wall again.

"God's chastising you, and it would be sinful for anyone to interfere in the chastisement!" He yelled, pulling me off the floor by my hair. I looked up at him, expecting the blows to start, thankful the children were in bed.

Then his hands dropped. He realized I wasn't crying.

For 14 years I had buckled to his abuse, always begging him not to hurt me. I feared an escalation of violence—furniture thrown across the room, hot tea in my face, black eyes, or worse.

But as I listened to him saying that God was punishing me, an inner voice started whispering, "He'll let you die, he'll let you die because he hates you."[1]

Domestic violence stretches around the world. Experts say it's reaching epidemic proportions. Former United States surgeon general C. Everett Coop labels it the "number-one health problem in America."[2] The American family and the American home are perhaps more violent than any other single American institution or setting with the exception of the military in time of war.[3] No segment of society is exempt from domestic violence. It knows no boundaries—religious, ethnic, or social.

Consider the following statistics:

- Domestic abuse is the most underreported crime in America—only 10 percent report.[4]
- According to a report from United States Senator Barbara Boxer on September 2, 1993, nine-tenths of all family violence defendants are never prosecuted, and one-third of the cases that would be considered felonies if committed by strangers are filed as misdemeanors (a lesser crime).
- Domestic violence is the leading cause of injuries to women ages 15 to 44, more common than auto accidents, muggings, rapes, and cancer deaths combined.[5]
- Every nine seconds a woman is battered.[6]
- In 24 to 30 percent of all homes violence occurs on a regular, ongoing basis.[7]
- Approximately 95 percent of victims of domestic violence are women.[8]
- Violence will occur at least once in 50 percent of all marriages.[9]
- Weapons are used in 30 percent of domestic violence incidents.[10]

- According to a report from the National Organization for Women, an average of 10 women per day are killed by their batterers.
- Women who leave their batterers are at a 75 percent greater risk of being killed by the batterer than are those who stay.
- Up to 50 percent of all homeless women and children in this country are fleeing domestic violence.[11]
- Violence is used by the perpetrator in a relationship as a means to gain control over the victim.[12]
- Of children who witness wife battering, 40 percent suffer anxiety, 48 percent suffer depression, 53 percent act out with parents, and 60 percent act out with siblings.[13]
- Current estimates of family violence in the United States suggest that three to five children in every classroom may witness violence in their homes.[14]
- Male children who witness adult-to-adult domestic violence are as adults 700 times more likely to beat their female partners. Male children who also are physically abused are as adults 1,000 times more likely to beat their female partners.[15]
- In a New York study of 50 battered women, 75 percent said they had been harassed by the batterer while they were at work, 50 percent reported missing an average of three days per month, and 44 percent lost at least one job for reasons directly related to the abuse.[16]
- Medical costs from domestic violence total at least $3 to $5 billion annually. At least another $100 million can be added to the cost to businesses in lost wages, sick leave, nonproductivity, and absenteeism (Porter, 1984).[17]
- Each year domestic violence leads to 100,000 days of hospitalization, 301,000 emergency room visits, and almost 40,000 visits to a physician.[18]

Surprisingly, the above statistics represent only physical

abuse, but family violence has many other expressions. In fact, domestic violence can range from a look to a gunshot.

Domestic abuse can range from a look to a gunshot.

DEFINING ABUSE

Every relationship has its ups and downs, and no marriage is completely free of conflict. But how do we know when normal conflict has crossed the line into dysfunction? The keys are to understand the parameters of healthy relationships and identify appropriate behaviors.

When a couple is not getting along and experiences conflicts that need to be resolved, both must recognize that the value of the relationship is greater than the conflict at hand. A primary tool in conflict resolution is to identify the problem and to attack the problem together rather than attacking each other.

Many unhealthy relationships lack this critical component. Instead, they resort to power and control, which manifests itself in many ways and takes forms that can be very subtle and difficult to pinpoint. Typically, an abusive partner will attempt significant control by exercising one or more of the following behaviors.

Physical Abuse

We have read in the newspaper and have seen on television many examples of physical abuse. You probably have an idea of what you consider abuse. However, physical abuse takes many forms: beating, biting, choking, grabbing, hitting, kicking, pinching, hair pulling, punching, pushing, restraining, scratching, shaking, shoving, slapping, excessive tickling, twisting arms, using weapons, spanking, and smothering.

Some men don't realize the extent of the pain they inflict because they don't recognize their own strength. Have you ever noticed a woman with quarter-size bruises on the inside of her arms? It's common for a male batterer to grab his partner by the upper arms to get her attention, shaking her while his adrenaline is pumping, and saying, "Listen to me!"

The woman may not even realize that she's bruised. If asked, the man would tell you, "I don't physically abuse her." One husband actually said, "I slapped her because I was trying to get her attention. She deserved it. If I beat her, she'd know it." This man defined beating as hitting with a closed fist. "I only slapped her—I didn't abuse her," he said.

When pressed, this man would tell you that he was out of control and didn't realize what he was doing. "She deserved it," he might say. Interesting, however, that he probably bruised her only in places where the bruises wouldn't show. He might be screaming, raging, and battering her, yet if someone phoned, he could answer the phone just as calm, cool, and collected as can be. "Hello? . . . How ya doin'? . . . Oh, I'm doing great!" The batterer has control to the point that he can go from one extreme to the other in seconds. Anytime he feels he has lost control of the woman or the situation, he resorts to some form of physical violence to regain control. It's a conscious effort.

> *A primary tool in confict resolution is to identify the problem and together attack the problem instead of each other.*

Power

Power manifests itself in many ways and can be a tool for abuse. In extreme cases, the husband may deny his wife the most basic necessities, such as food or sleep. Or she may be denied a private life of her own.

In this type of abuse, the man mandates the woman's duties. She knows when and what she is supposed to cook, when she's supposed to do the laundry, and when she's supposed to wash the car. He regiments her life. He may even control the amount of bath water she uses. He feels he has the right to teach her a lesson, even to the extent of trying to exert his power by saying something like "She was acting like a child, so I turned her over my knee."

PHYSICAL ABUSE
Exhibited by beating, biting, choking, grabbing, hitting, kicking, pinching, pulling hair, punching, pushing, restraining, scratching, shaking, shoving, slapping, excessive tickling, twisting arms, using weapons, spanking, smothering, tripping

MALE PRIVILEGE
Treats victim like a servant; makes all the decisions; acts like "Master of the Castle"

KNOWLEDGE ABUSE
Gets therapy, goes to seminars, uses self-help books then comes back and abuses with the knowledge he has but doesn't take responsibility for personal behaviors

SEXUAL ABUSE
Demands unwanted or bizarre sexual acts; physical attacks to sexual parts of the body; treats her as a sex object; interrupts sleep for sex; forces sex; exhibits extreme jealousy

HUMILIATION
Hostile humor; publicly humiliates; criticizes; degrades her appearance, her parenting skills, her housekeeping, cooking, etc; forces her to eat foods she doesn't like

RESPONSIBILITY ABUSE
Makes victim responsible for everything in life, i.e., bills, parenting, etc.

MEDICAL ABUSE
Hurts her and does not allow her to receive medical treatment; does not allow her to receive medical treatment for normal health issues

RELIGIOUS ABUSE
Uses Scripture and words like "submission" and "obey" to abuse; spiritual language

USING CHILDREN
Uses the children to give messages; uses visitation rights to harass; uses child support as leverage

POWER AND CONTROL

ISOLATION
Controls what is done, who is seen, who it talked to; limits or listens in on phone calls; sabotages car; restricts outside interests; insists on moving frequently; requires her to stay in the house; restricts access to the mail; deprives her of friends

POWER
Denies basic rights; uses the law to enforce his power; deprives her of a private or personal life; mandates duties; controls everything, i.e., the amount of bath water she uses

STALKING
Spies on her, follows her to activities, i.e., store, church, work, etc. Displays extreme distrust and jealousy

EMOTIONAL ABUSE
Puts her down; calls her names; plays mind games; commits mental coercion; exhibits extreme controlling behaviors; withholds affection; causes her to lose her identity

THREATS
Threatens to end the relationship; threatens to emotionally or physically harm her; threatens her life; threatens to take the children, commit suicide, report her to authorities; forces her to break the law.

ECONOMIC ABUSE
Puts restriction on her employment; makes her ask for money; gives her an allowance and takes the money she earns; requires her to account for every penny she spends

FINANCIAL ABUSE
Ruins her credit; puts cars, house, recreational equipment, and/or property in his name; spends her money, uses her credit or savings to make her dependent on him

INTIMIDATION
Uses looks, actions, gestures, and voice to cause fear; argues continuously; demands that victim says what he wants to hear

PROPERTY VIOLENCE
Punches walls, destroys property, breaks down doors, pounds tables, abuses pets, etc.

VERBAL ABUSE
Curses, accuses, name-calls, uses past to control and manipulate, commits mental blackmail, makes unreasonable demands

SILENCE
Uses silence as a weapon; does not communicate; does not express emotion

Stalking

Stalking is similar to spying. The stalker may follow his victim to her activities or while she's running errands. He doesn't trust her and is insanely jealous. *If I can't have her, no one can*, he thinks. Most people think that stalking is limited to relationships characterized by separation or divorce, but it happens also in marriage relationships. It applies to many couples—even Christian couples—where the husband is insecure. Often the wife has no idea that the stalking is occurring.

Technology has opened the door to some new and interesting ways of stalking one's partner. There have been cases of a stalker purchasing a GPS transmitter and hiding it in his victim's car, thus tracking her with his receiver.

Computers are also utilized in stalking. We counseled a man who had filed for divorce yet had more information about his wife after their separation than he did before. When I confronted him, I determined that he had made contact with her in a chat room. Pretending to be a sympathetic female shoulder to cry on, he was able to find out her salary on her new job, who her friends were, who she was seeing, and what she and her dates were doing. This information fed his jealousy, and it was necessary for the wife to get a restraining order and move to a safe place in another area for her own protection.

We once counseled a woman whose life was in jeopardy, and she had moved from California to the Midwest. Within 30 days her former husband traced her to her new address on his computer. His first search was of the California Department of Motor Vehicles records. Most states require individuals to register their vehicles and transfer license plates within 30 days of moving to another state. This man was also able to search for and find her address through the utility companies. Listed below are some of the searches a partner may utilize to find a partner who has moved to a safe place. Victims should be aware and use extreme care when it's necessary to keep their whereabouts secret.

- Department of Motor Vehicles

- Utility companies
- Social Security number
- United States Postal Service
- Telephone company
- Credit reporting agencies
- Driver's license bureaus

Stalking is the most difficult slice of the power and control wheel to deal with because law enforcement can't arrest until the damage has been done. We recommend that the stalking victim seek an "order of protection" or a "no contact order." If one of these is in place and the stalker refuses to honor it and keeps calling, the victim should get an answering machine that records the unanswered phone calls and keeps a record. If the stalker drives by her home or workplace or follows her in her daily routine, she needs to report and record every conversation with the police department, asking for names and badge numbers to document the call on the tape. This should include the time and date of the infraction. There should be an extensive paper trail for the victim's protection.

Emotional Abuse

Emotional abuse happens when a man puts a woman down and makes her feel bad about herself. He might call her names. He might try to make her think she's crazy. He plays mind games with her. His behaviors eventually control her life, perhaps to the point that she's not able to have friends.

At first his control may seem like genuine concern. If the woman comes from a family situation in which her emotional needs were not met, she may be particularly vulnerable. A man comes into her life, and he wants to get involved. He might make a car payment for her or perhaps buy her a piece of furniture. He calls her several times a day at work, and she feels for the first time there is somebody who really loves her. She doesn't recognize the symptoms of a controlling man who is immature and has the potential to abuse her. Because of the neglect in her family of origin, she sees all of this attention as love. She sees it as a connection. She sees it as a blessing. It feels great to have somebody care about her bills, about where she lives, about her having a piece of furniture, enough about her to send her flowers or to give her $50.

Then they marry, and she can't even have $3 to purchase a personal item or two. It's all part of the game. The moment he has her secured (that is, they marry or move in together or have sex), he "owns" her. He changes. What brought her into that relationship felt like love and concern but becomes the very curse she can't get away from. He makes her feel like a hostage, giving her affection only under certain conditions. She may be denied physical needs, such as food and sleep, and he deprives her of identity development or autonomy. He demands that she meet his every need and satisfy his every whim.

Threats

Sometimes the man threatens his partner about ending their relationship. "You're lucky you have me," he says. "You're going to find out it's a tough world out there without me." She perceives this as a threat because he has made her so dependent upon him. This dynamic is called "learned helplessness."

If this technique is unsuccessful, the man may intensify his efforts. He declares that he'll do something to hurt her emotionally or physically. He may threaten her life or say he'll take the children. He might even threaten to commit suicide. To a woman in a state of learned helplessness, it seems she has no way out. He threatens to report her to the authorities or remove her financial support. He could force her or set her up to break the law by asking her to write a bad check, charge something on someone else's credit card, or steal. Then he uses that as leverage to keep her from leaving by threatening to call the police and tell them what she did. Of course, she feels trapped.

Another form of control can come as a result of morality issues. "If you really love me," he might say, "you'll sleep with my friend." Perhaps he beats her until she complies, and he brings a third party into their bedroom. He could then hold her behavior over her head and threaten that if she ever tries to leave him, there will be a witness that she was immoral. She fears that if she ever stands up to him the children will be taken away from her and placed with him.

A woman who has either broken the law or been involved with a third party in the bedroom lives in constant fear because she has been set up. She wonders if and when her husband will tell. She is in bondage to his power and control and feels that she cannot or dare not escape. In an extremely violent family, this is very commonplace.

Economic Abuse

An economic abuser will likely try to keep his wife from getting a job or keeping a job. He will usually make her ask or beg for money. He takes any money she earns and gives her an allowance, making her account for every penny she spends.

A man who employs this means of abuse will perhaps give his wife $50 and tell her to go to the store and get groceries for a family of four for the week. With the $50 in hand, his last words ring in her ears—"Bring back the change and the receipt." She must carefully calculate every purchase. She unloads her shopping cart and fearfully waits for the total. If it's $51.45, she begins to panic as she realizes she forgot to allow for tax. She stands there with a line behind her, embarrassed and angry with herself for her stupidity. She stammers to the clerk as she tries to figure out what to put back. "I guess I don't need this right now." The clerk rolls his eyes. She's humiliated and feels stung by his look. Then a voice in the back of the line blurts out, "I always pick the wrong line. That dumb lady up there . . ." She's humiliated even more. This woman often sacrifices her own needs for the needs and wants of her family. It seems there's no way out because there's no financial vehicle for escape.

Financial Abuse

Financial abuse differs from economic abuse. We have counseled many men—and this seems to be a "guy thing"— where the abuser has used the woman's credit to purchase items in his name only. These purchases range from stereo equipment, cars, motorcycles, boats, etc. One man bought a house using her credit. He forged her signature and had it notarized by his friend. He then put the home in his name only and moved his girlfriend into it. When the wife discovered what he had done, she had to hire an attorney and spend time and money to rectify the situation. Often the end result is that he moves on, but her credit is ruined, and she suffers to get back on her feet financially for several years.

We have also seen instances of men draining their wives of any money they may have inherited in order to keep them financially dependent.

Intimidation

When a man intimidates his wife to the point that it's abusive behavior, he puts fear into her by using looks, actions, gestures, a loud voice, cursing, and continual arguing. The woman learns that she must say to him what he wants to hear. She soon learns exactly what it is that he wants to hear so that she can placate and acquiesce to him. He wants her to listen to him with undivided attention. He demands that she report to him. Remember—domestic violence can range from a look to a gunshot.

If something triggers the temper of a man who abuses by intimidation, he starts screaming, raging, and cursing. The wife tries to keep peace because she's embarrassed by what's going on. He's being childish, like a four-year-old having a tantrum. He's never learned how to resolve conflict and is willing to disrupt the whole world to get his way at any cost.

Property Violence

Abusive behavior that qualifies as property violence includes behaviors such as punching walls, smashing belongings, and generally destroying property. Surprisingly, the man who chooses property violence is normally in control of his rage. He doesn't throw his socket set through the front window—it's her china, her tapes, or something else that's precious to her.

Breaking down doors, pounding tables, and abusing pets are all property violence. This man may even kill the family pet because it shows the amount of power he thinks he possesses. The subconscious message he is trying to convey to his children is that Dad has power over life and death—so the family often wonders if and when they'll be next. (If this is happening, there needs to be a separation, and the family should be taken to a safe place. The primary goal in a domestic violence situation is the safety of the wife and children. With the man, containment of the behavior is primary.)

Knowledge Abuse

A little knowledge can be devastating when used in the wrong way. If a man continues to deny his wrongdoing and continually blames his partner, the counseling he receives can be turned on her, and he will use it against her.

One example of this would be: The man reads a book on premenstrual syndrome (PMS). He researches the subject and attacks her with his knowledge, saying, "If it weren't for your PMS, we would have a good marriage. It's all your fault. Go get help now. I don't need counseling." Again, she is responsible for all of his problems, and he has no empathy for her situation. He may go to counseling once or twice, telling the counselor about her problems. She stays in therapy, thinks she's crazy, and he wins again.

A man like this often seeks a counselor he can fool. He reads self-help books and adapts the information to his partner. Sometimes he finds a pastor who sides with him on submission and then spiritually batters his wife with that information. He also may use the opinions of unqualified friends to control her. It sounds like this: "Even your friend Linda and her husband agree with me." Last, he will go to his own family—especially his mother—and then parrot their opinions and suggestions to abuse and control his wife.

Medical Abuse

I received an e-mail recently that said, "As I was looking

over your web site, something occurred to me. There isn't a 'slice' for medical abuse in the power and control wheel." Many times a physically abusive partner will break a bone and then not let the woman go to the doctor for help. I have talked to many victims who have let broken toes, fingers, and other injuries, heal without seeing a physician. They bore the pain because they knew the doctor is mandated to report bruises, broken bones, and domestic rape. Domestic violence is a crime. On the other side of the pendulum is a woman who suffers with medical problems not necessarily caused by abuse, but they are real. She is then blamed, harassed, and abused with no sympathy or empathy. He has no patience for her needs and sees her needs as infringement on his rights, his time, and his finances.

Judy: *Once when I was painting a ceiling, I saw a small spot that I had missed. I climbed back on the ladder and put one foot on a desk for balance. I took a hard fall onto the desk, knocking the wind out of myself. I was in a lot of pain, but I didn't have a car so I waited until Paul came home that evening. I told him what had happened and that I thought I might really have hurt myself because the pain was getting worse. He yelled at me and told me I was an idiot because I should not have been so stupid as to stand on the desk in the first place. I asked him to take me to the emergency room, and he was angry that I didn't just walk to the hospital because he was tired from working all day, and this was an inconvenience. I finally convinced him to take me to the ER, and found that I had five broken ribs. Paul could not have cared less— I had wasted his evening.*

Silent Knight

Some men use silence as a weapon. A man who does this cannot or will not communicate and often lacks the abilities or mechanisms to express his emotions. Typically he pays the bills, attends church, and is seen by others as a solid Christian. He is the kind of man who is consistent on his job and with his friends. He does not appear to be an angry or violent man. He never degrades his wife, hits her, or threatens her. She does not live in fear.

There comes a time, however, that she becomes depressed. She asks herself, *What's wrong with me? I have a good husband and a good life. Why am I so depressed? My husband treats me well. He pays the bills, he's stable, he's solid, he's a Christian. Why do I have this hollow feeling inside of me?* Her friends tell her that she is fortunate to have such a good husband; yet she still feels there's something missing.

By nature, when something goes wrong in a man's world, he looks outward to blame someone, something, or a circumstance. A woman, however, is more sensitive and looks inward for answers. She begins to question herself: *What's wrong with me? Why won't he pay attention to me?* She knows she's missing something, but she may not recognize what it is. She doesn't consciously know that she is being cheated of emotional bonding.

He has not involved himself in her life. She sees his lack of interest as an indication that she is unworthy of his attention. It's difficult for her to put into words. She may ask herself again, *What's wrong with me?* She begins searching for an answer by criticizing her body. *Am I too fat? Am I too thin? Do I have a bad body? Is my nose too big? Am I getting wrinkles? Do I need plastic surgery?*

After she agonizes over her appearance, she begins to dissect her sexuality. *Maybe I don't respond to him properly. He must not like the way I make love. I don't satisfy him.* She then looks outside her person. *Is it the house? Don't I keep a nice home? Is it my cooking? Did I produce ugly children? Maybe I didn't produce the kind of children he wanted.*

After living with this self-doubt for an extended period, she draws a line at the bottom of all of the questions and answers, *It's all of the above.* She doesn't do this consciously; however, she assumes that every doubt she has about herself is true. The lack of his response and emotional bonding tells her that she's the problem.

I have asked men, "How do you emotionally connect with your wife?" They can't tell me. There's not a course called "Intimacy 101" to train men how to connect emotionally.

If a man falls into this category of being a "silent knight" and the couple approaches their pastor or a counselor, generally the wife will say, "We love each other, we're committed to each other, but something's missing."

The husband will often say, "Everything's fine. She must be in depression."

The pastor may ask, "Is there any physical abuse in the relationship?"

She responds, "No. He's never been inappropriate with me in any way."

"Is there emotional abuse?"

"No, never." There is nothing on the power-and-control list that makes sense. The pastor then refers them to a therapist. They still find no answers. The therapist often wants to see the woman for further counseling. She once again thinks she's crazy, that it's her fault and her problem.

I sometimes counsel groups of men to work on their abilities to bond emotionally. I ask them, "How do you make love to your wife?" Their answers always end with sex.

"How do you make love emotionally to your wife?"

"I pay the bills and I buy her the things she needs."

They have no concept of what it means to invest emotionally in their partners. When a man becomes aware of a woman's emotional needs, it begins the process of learning to look her in the eye, listen to her, and validate her feelings. She gets his undivided attention.

The next step is to teach the man how to get in touch with his feelings. Nothing bonds a couple together more than for the man to share his inner feelings and to acknowledge his weaknesses. When he trusts her enough to share his feelings, dreams, and goals, she knows the trust factor between them is building. She feels worthy because in their relationship he has invested a listening ear as well as nonsexual touching.

One reason women avoid approaching their husbands for a simple hug is because many men interpret the request for a hug as a signal for sex. When a man learns that a hug can be simply a signal for closeness and that his wife should be able to ask for a hug and not be groped, the couple has reached a new level of emotional bonding. When she knows that he loves her for who she is without physical gratification, she feels connected. A man, then, can learn that the greatest intimacy in a relationship is the disclosure of himself. The relationship then becomes safe without the fear of rejection.

Isolation

When a man controls what his wife does, who she sees, who she talks to, and where she goes, it is classified as abuse through isolation. He probably limits her phone conversations. When she does talk on the phone, he listens in. He might try to isolate her from her family. He insists on knowing where she is at all times, and she must be available to him at all times.

Women who are abused in this way are usually not allowed to have interests outside their homes, and this is emphasized by frequent moves —from house to house and town to town. He may even move her away from her family so that she has no support system. To keep her in isolation, he might leave her without any means of transportation or else sabotage her car. Often she's not even allowed to open the mail.

There is nothing that will bond a couple together more than for the man to share his inner feelings and acknowledge his weaknesses.

Using Children

A husband can make his wife feel guilty about various aspects of raising their children, especially if his behavior includes using the children to inflict abuse on their mother. He may use the children to convey indirect messages to his wife. If the couple is no longer married, he might use visitation (or lack of it) as harassment. Or maybe he uses child support as leverage. Even if the couple is divorced and remarried to others, where there are children and money involved, the abuse can go on and on.

There are instances in which the divorced father will

come to get the children for the weekend and return them on Sunday night with the kids bouncing off the walls. It takes Mom most of the week to get the kids pasted back together again, and then the cycle starts all over on Friday night. There's never a moment's peace, because one parent uses the children to control the life of the other.

Humiliation

A form of abuse that includes certain kinds of humor, public humiliation, verbal criticism, and inappropriate touching in public is the abusive behavior of humiliation.

By inappropriately touching her in public, the husband is letting the world know that his wife belongs to him. "She's my possession. I own her. She's part of my inventory."

He'll no doubt discredit her appearance, her parenting skills, her housekeeping, her cooking, and her self-worth. He probably insists that she dress to suit him. With this type of abuse the man is insecure and wants to prove that she is his. He may see his wife as a trophy and therefore want her to dress in sexy clothing, even if it degrades and humiliates her. The irony is, after he puts her down and degrades her, he'll want to go to bed with her.

Responsibility Abuse

In responsibility abuse the husband makes his wife feel responsible for everything in his life—like bills and children. He may threaten to commit suicide in order to make her feel responsible for his very life. He could even put his wife in a mothering, caretaking, nurturing role. Usually in this situation the husband will insist that the wife make major decisions, but then he punishes her for the decision she made—even if it was correct.

Spiritual Abuse

Words like "submission" and "obey," as well as other spiritual language and scripture, are taken out of context by the man who spiritually abuses his wife. He probably has high regard for the patriarchal system and says things like "God gives me the right to do this. I'm the head of the family. I have all the rights in the world, and you have none."

I once knew a man who was so physically abusive and spiritually toxic that he literally beat his wife with the Bible. She moved out and got a restraining order against him. He broke into the home, took the big family Bible, hit her over the head, and said, "The pastor said that this family would be intact if you would come under total submission like the Bible says." He quoted scripture to her after putting her in the hospital with two dislocated vertebrae. That's spiritual abuse. The pastor, perhaps unknowingly, was giving the husband permission to abuse his wife spiritually and physically. Women who have experienced this type of abuse often feel that God loves men but that women have no place in the world. Judy, my own wife, struggled in her relationship with God because of the way I physically and spiritually abused her. I battered her, then stepped behind the pulpit half an hour later. When she was in her greatest need she sought counseling at the church she was attending but couldn't get an appointment with the pastor or Christian counselor. The pastor wouldn't meet with her because she was divorced. The Christian counselor wouldn't meet with her because she didn't have any money. Where are we in the Body of Christ when it comes to helping hurting women?

Sexual Abuse

Men who abuse their partners often want to have sex with them soon after they assault them. We have a saying: "Domestic violence is not foreplay." Under the auspices of her proving her faithfulness and love, a sexually abusive man may insist his partner perform bizarre sexual acts against her will. Sometimes he actually physically attacks the sexual parts of her body or treats her as a sex object. He might also withhold sex or interrupt her sleep for sex. If she declines his offers, he threatens to find someone who will satisfy his fantasies. He may force sex, commit marital rape, and be extremely jealous.

When earlier defining the abuse of "threats," I mentioned the situation of the husband asking his wife to go to bed with another person. This gives him leverage if she ever fails to do as he wishes. This is also considered sexual abuse.

A sexually abusive man may get so angry that he hits his wife with a closed fist in the most sensitive areas on her body. He may pinch and squeeze her breasts until it's unbearable. Of course, this can cause permanent damage.

Just weeks before I finished the manuscript for this book, a man was arrested in Colorado for tying his wife up and burning her with a butane torch. Consider Gloria, whose husband poured acid into her feminine hygiene products and burned her so badly that she can never have intercourse again. It's very common for a sexually abusive man to disfigure his wife's genital area. He thinks, "If I can't have her, I'm going to fix her so nobody will want her if she even tries to present herself to another man."

Using Male Privilege

A man who treats "his woman" like a servant, makes all the big decisions, and acts like the master of the castle is exerting a type of abuse known as male privilege. Do you have an "Archie Bunker" chair in your house? Who has the television remote in your house? It's more of a guy thing.

One of our Life Skills directors, a 24-year law enforcement veteran, was recently teaching a workshop in which he talked about male privilege. One of the police officers came back the next morning and said,

> I have to share a story with you. I have an Archie Bunker chair. I went home last night and told my wife to burn the chair, reupholster the chair, give the chair away, sit in the chair, jump in the chair—do whatever she wanted to—because I'm changing. I'm going to spend some time with my family.
>
> My routine was that I would go home from work worn

out, sit in my chair, kick back, turn the TV on, ask my kids to bring me a drink, and wait for my wife to bring me supper. Normally I fell asleep in the chair, I woke up after everyone had gone to bed, I got up to go to bed, and that would be my evening. Last night I had supper with my kids and my wife, and it was delightful. I was in the kitchen. I told my wife she could do anything she wanted to do with the chair. We had a great time, except I have two German shepherds, and for the last seven years they have sat on each side of my chair while I sat there. Dad wasn't in his chair last night, so the dogs went ballistic. If the dogs were that disrupted over my routine, what has my family been feeling in this area of male privilege?

Not all of abuses are committed by men only. During the 23 years that Life Skills has existed, we have found that a woman who was abused as a child or has been in an abusive relationship will feel that if abuse worked for him, maybe it will work for her too. She holds to the old adage "Fight fire with fire." The woman then fights back for her survival; she is called the "reactive victim." But where one is teachable, these behaviors are fixable. There is hope.

Chapter 3

IT'S ALL IN
YOUR HEAD

It's important to understand the neurobiology of the brain
and how it works. There are at least five things that can happen to a child that will cause arrested development. A child
can be traumatized through rejection, incest, molestation,
emotional abuse, or physical abuse. I have listed these in the
order of severity. The wounds of these traumas cause changes
in the neurobiology of the child.

One of my mentors, the late Eldon Chalmers, spent 39
years mapping the brain, looking at the chemical structure of
the brain and how it works when traumatized. He studied
how the brain works when one is feeling happy, sad, or experiencing other emotions. He shared this information with me
years ago, and I started using his discoveries in my teaching,
even though I was criticized at the time. I didn't let the criticism stop me, and in the last three to five years there has
been tremendous research in this area. Bessel Van Der Koke
has written a very helpful book on the subject, titled *Traumatic Stress.*

The brain works much like a miniature computer. Computers are hard-wired—printed circuit boards. The brain is
made up of chemical electrical impulses. It would require a
building 100 stories tall and the size of the state of Texas to
house a computer that could replicate some of what the human brain does. The brain is "voice activated," so we don't
need keyboards. Information comes into our brains through
sound, sight, smell, touch, and taste.

Our "computer" never forgets; it is so magnificently created that every word spoken is retained. Our computer keeps a record of every word spoken from the first noises we uttered as babies. In Psalms 139, the scripture tells us that God knows every word we have spoken to this day and even more; He knows every word we have in us yet to speak. Think about that.

God says that if we curse someone, we're cursing ourselves. If we bless someone, we're blessing ourselves. In other words, if I speak a blessing or curse to someone, then that which comes out of my mouth not only goes to that person but also comes back and goes into my "computer."

Because of the sin nature and the wounds of childhood, we have been programmed negatively. When we become angry and fly into a rage, not understanding how we're wired, something is triggered within us, and we speak, we curse, we gripe, we complain, and we murmur. That is why the Scriptures make so much of the spoken word. What we say we will receive.

One thing we must not fail to understand is that if someone is abusing us, we have the right to remove ourselves from that situation. We have the right to counseling, to share what's going on—but we don't curse the abuser. The Scriptures say that you bless those who despitefully use you. That's how important the spoken word is, because when we speak it, we hear it. When we speak it long enough the subconscious —or the heart—will come into submission to what is spoken. The way the mind works is that when we receive information we perceive it before we receive it.

If you have been wounded in childhood, your perception is that your world is not safe. Another perception is that you are flawed, defective, dirty, damaged, and different. I sometimes use the illustration of a furnace filter. Coming into your computer is a filtering system that gathers in all of the injustice, all of the wounds of childhood, and holds those there in a violation column. That violation column, until it is dealt with, will keep gathering injustice, wounds, rejection, and everything that comes in that is negative. It will hold it all there and become your *perception*—and that becomes your *re-*

ality. Any *truth* then must travel through this clogged filtering system.

Let's use an example of a woman who was abused during childhood and has come to me for counseling. I might say to her, "That is a beautiful sweater you're wearing." Her immediate response is "It's nothing special; I only got it at a discount store." It's hard for her to take a compliment because of the previous wounding in her childhood. If I say something positive or complimentary, she wonders about my agenda. Because of what she experienced in childhood and because of the developmental arrests at the stage of where the wounds occurred, she regresses to child. What I said went through her filtering system, and she didn't hear *reality*. She heard her *perception*. It's important to deal with this.

Here's an example of one of the most traumatic times in my life:

I was 13 years old when my father took a pastorate in a small community. On my first day in junior high in my new school, I went into the science class. The teacher asked if there was anyone who would like to go help in the photography darkroom. I was interested in photography, and I was the new kid, so I volunteered. I didn't know that trauma was waiting for me behind those doors. Just as I was rolling the film into the developing tank, the student teacher molested me. I had been molested previously, so I froze. I couldn't move. When I came out of that darkroom, I thought every student in the class and the teacher knew what had happened. I was humiliated beyond words. Because of my embarrassment and the fact that I was violated, I started acting out in rage and anger. When I would go to the homes of my friends I would look for opportunities to go through their parents' nightstands and other belongings looking for a gun. I vowed that if I found one I would take it to school and kill that student teacher. I knew what had happened to me, but nobody else knew it. It was an overwhelming relief when my dad told me we were going to move away.

In our communications, we hear through our filters—our

perceptions of what someone is trying to tell us. Truth is not received as truth and reality—it's received as perception.

In the example from my life, what I meant to communicate couldn't get through my guilt and shame and humiliation because of what had happened to me. The brain sorts information through its filtering system. The raw incoming data is perceived before it is received, so the brain perceives, receives, sorts, analyzes, compares, catalogs, files, retrieves, utilizes, determines, and chooses. When the filtering system is filled with traumatic wounds that clog our perceptions, it keeps us from seeing reality. One who is wounded in this way tries to communicate, tries to love, tries to resolve conflict and manage his or her anger as normal, healthy adults do. The person knows what's right and knows what should be done but can't see reality or truth and can't resolve his or her conflicts because it can't get through the filtering system. Now that person is limited in two ways. He or she doesn't see reality—only the perception of everything that happens and things said in conversation—and the person can't communicate truth or feelings. Because those perceptions aren't dealt with and conflicts aren't resolved, the person gets frustrated and lives in a rage. That is how the brain works.

The amygdale is a gland located in the brain and is attached to the hippocampus, yet wired directly to the thalamus. The amygdale is the shape and size of an almond, 1½ inches inside of each temple. The amygdale is wired to the thalamus, which is like a train-switching station. When trauma occurs, the thalamus responds automatically to the danger or threat and takes control of the situation by eliminating all thinking processes, literally hijacking the brain, and we then react. Then there is a shot of adrenaline that surges through the body and raises the blood pressure, creates fear, creates sadness, and alerts the survival instinct. That's the function of the amygdale.

Let's look at two scenarios:

First, let's use as an example a little boy who has never been wounded and is somewhat trusting, and whose life is going fairly well. The software says to this child subconsciously, *You have value; you're worthy of acceptance; you're worthy of love; you're worthy of nurture; you're worthy of being taken care of; and you're worthy of being touched properly.*

Next let's think about a little boy who has been rejected and sexually, emotionally, or physically abused. These wounds create powerlessness, and because of this powerlessness, this child finds himself in a situation that he didn't see coming and that he can't control. This child is now in a situation that is foreign to the software in his brain. At this point this child knows the difference between a proper touch and an improper touch. His subconscious knows the difference, and the subconscious can tell the difference between something that not right and something that's right, even though he is not cognitive of what's happening. That's how the human brain is wired. This child is being abused and caught off guard. He thought his world was safe and that all people should respect him. When the abusive incident occurred, it went directly against everything in the software. This is a trauma.

The trauma creates a single synaptic neuronal connector directly to the amygdala. It is like a power surge that creates fear. From that point forward, for the rest of the child's life, any event that even remotely resembles that trauma will cause the amygdala to respond. The child could walk into a dark house on a sunny day, and the darkness of the place will trigger the memory of trauma. That subconscious response will cause the child to be afraid of something he is not consciously aware of, and that will trigger the amygdala.

The thalamus received the input and tells the input where to go. If I'm having a good time and I'm in conversation with someone and experiencing joy and peace, all the input from that goes through the thalamus, and the thalamus routes it to the frontal lobe. The frontal lobe is where we think, decide, feel emotions, choose, communicate, and build intimacy. If something happens that has the feel of an unsafe situation, it triggers danger that goes to the thalamus and the thalamus routes it to the amygdala instantly. The amygdala is the one

gland in the brain that causes the reactive behavior so that
we react instantly—without thinking. The amygdala literally
hijacks the thinking process of the brain, and the child is not
even aware of his reaction many times.

When the little boy we're using as an example is 50 years
old, if something triggers him, he will react before thinking.
Because he's developmentally frozen or arrested in childhood,
the amygdala hijacks the thinking processes of the brain, and
he regresses back to his emotional childhood.

The amygdala then sends the signal to the adrenaline
gland. The adrenaline gland is on top of the kidneys. Have
you ever come close to having an accident and pulled off the
road with your head spinning and your back hurting? Your
back hurts because of the instant surge of adrenaline. Adrenaline does not surge on a daily basis because we were meant to
live in peace and to resolve our conflicts. Adrenaline was giv-
en so that when we are in danger we will either fight to the
death or flee. That's the survival technique built into human
beings, and it's called the fight/flight syndrome.

Fight/flight works in emotionally healthy people. But the
adrenaline glands of the man wounded in childhood secrete
adrenaline, and he is paralyzed and can't fight and can't run.
Arrested development, or the wounds of childhood, paralyze
the survival instinct.

It can be sexual abuse, physical abuse, or rejection that arrests the development and rewires the amygdala. But when
something happens and the world doesn't look safe, the
abused individual is paralyzed and emotionally returns to the
point of trauma.

When this child was wounded, it was wired to the amygdala. When he suffers another wound, it goes through the
same wiring, and when he is triggered it goes through the
same wiring. It's a lot like taking an extension cord and slic-
ing it the long way so that the wiring is exposed. It's then
wired directly from the senses to the thalamus and directly to
the amygdala, and it causes this boy to react for his lifetime.

The Creator has given us free will, and we can change the

wiring of the brain by the choice of our will, but the change takes about 36 months. During that 36 months we will develop delayed responses that become impulse control. Healing is not just an emotional thing—it is literally rewiring the brain. And that takes time.

The thalamus is the train-switching station that routes our pain and impulses through the hippocampus into the amygdala, and the amygdala is right there to react so that we can survive.

The body has cell memory. It can be an image we see (the visual); what we hear (audio); or it can be how we're touched. I worked with a client whose father had molested her when she was 6 or 7 years old, and when he did this, he put the heel of his hand in the small of her back. Fifty years later, each time her husband touched the small of her back she went to pieces. She asked me once, "Will the day ever come that the man I love can touch me in that place and it not trigger me in a bizarre way?" She reacted in this way because of the programming in her subconscious mind—the database.

Touch, taste, smell, sound, what we see—all can trigger and then hijack the frontal lobes of the brain. The thalamus receives the stimulus and shunts it to the amygdala. The amygdala kicks out the adrenaline, and we react with anger, rage, and fear because of our survival technique. Fear and anger tell us that something is wrong in our world, and that causes us to go into survival mode. If we have been wounded as children and never resolved the issues, the survival instinct is the mode we react to. This creates rage and fear. We want to strike back, to get even, and we want to protect ourselves spiritually, emotionally, and physically.

There is a healing process, though, and a way to reroute the way the brain works. We can learn to rewire around our issues, delay our responses, and be able to use the frontal lobe thinking abilities and choose our behavior instead of reacting.

Trauma frightens us so much that it etches the single wiring connector from our senses to the amygdala itself. It is im-

portant to recognize what happens as result of being fright-
ened as a child.

The brain stores trauma in a different way than it does daily
emotional events. Happy things and even sad things go into
the brain differently than traumatic memories. This is called
narrative memory. Traumatic memories store themselves in a
cluster and go directly to the brain in vivid color. Normal
memories have a tendency to fade in time, but traumatic memory etches into the brian deeply and in such a way that when
something triggers that memory, the memory becomes intrusive. It can be recalled many years later with the same emotion,
intensity, and fear that was experienced when it occurred.

Researchers have done scans and found that when a traumatic memory is triggered, the brain will light up just as if
that event just happened. That is why intrusive memories become a crisis for us. When the intrusive memory occurs and it
has not been resolved or put to rest in the subconscious, it
triggers the amygdala in hopes that this time the traumatic
incident will be dealt with and resolved. You cannot stop a
traumatic memory. You can be thinking about a birthday party you had when you were a child, and in the middle of
thinking about that your mind flits off to something else.
That's normal memory. We have the choice to move from
memory to memory. If something triggers us, we can't stop
that intrusive memory from coming out. It's going to come
out, raise our blood pressure, and come out in the full emotions. That's why it's intrusive and we become reactive to it.
Remember that narrative memory is normal and that traumatic memory is intrusive. That's why over a number of years
traumatic memory fires our burners and we can explode in
anger and rage. The amygdala is basically programmed to respond to danger and not much else. When we were wounded
and caught off guard as children, those memories went into
memory banks and weren't dealt with.

The wounds cause the amygdala to raise the trip wire.
When we are wounded again, the trip wire rises more. When
we are wounded again and again and nothing gets resolved,

the multiple wounds in childhood keep raising the trip wire, and the fuse becomes extremely short. By adulthood it seems that anything can trip us up, and we'll trigger, freak out, escalate, get angry, and start cursing, raging, and reacting.

Children are often wounded below the age of communication and below the age of language. I have been dealing for years with men who are really men of God, some of them pastors and people in high level business who wonder why they struggle with cursing, anger, and rage. They love Jesus more than anything and have given their lives to him, but when they go into a rage they start cursing. I have found that if you have been wounded below the age of language and you're triggered, you do not have the mechanisms to deal with the resolution of the problem or expression of what is happening. This send you into survival mode and all you can do is curse and rage.

As I mentioned earlier, "If you are teachable, it's all fixable." We have learned in our research that people can deal with what they can understand and what they don't understand drives them crazy. It is the unknown in life that drives behaviors. Remember, as you read on that once you see that the attitudes and behaviors we struggle with are rooted or sourced in early childhood wounds, the brain starts the process of recovery. The brain will file the pain in the proper folders in the software and start the resolution of the conflicts of childhood. With the proper information in place and the loose ends tied together, the subconscious then sees that we are not flawed or defective. Remember, there is always a reason for these types of behaviors. Anger, rage, violence, fear, and anxiety do not come from a vacuum. There is always a reason, but never an *excuse*. Thus there is *hope* and *help* for those who are hurting.

Chapter 4

IDENTIFYING ABUSE

Who's doing all this battering? You may notice that all the examples we use are of men battering women. That's because 95 percent of all family violence involves men against women.[1] Although they come from all socioeconomic levels and every occupation, batterers and their victims have characteristics that make them fairly easy to identify.

COMMON CHARACTERISTICS OF THE MAN WHO BATTERS

- He has low self-esteem.
- He believes all the myths about battering relationships.
- He is a traditionalist who believes in male supremacy and the stereotypical masculine sex role in the family. He feels he has the right to "teach her a lesson."
- He blames others for his actions.
- He has exaggerated jealousy. In order for him to feel secure, he must become overinvolved in his wife's life. Often he makes her account for every moment of her time. Despite constant surveillance, he is still suspicious of every relationship she has with other men and women. Frequently there is verbal abuse about suspected affairs.
- He exhibits a dual personality.
- He has severe stress reactions during which he uses drinking and/or wife-beating to cope.
- He uses sex as an aggressive act to enhance his self-esteem in view of waning virility.

- He does not believe that his violent behavior should have any negative consequences.
- He typically denies that the couple has a problem and becomes enraged if his partner reveals the true situation.
- He has an element of overkill. He overdoes things, both while battering (cannot seem to control the brutal attack) and when in a loving period (showers partner with affection, attention, and gifts).
- He came from a violent home. He either saw his father beat his mother or was himself battered.
- His relationship with his mother was unusual. Often there was an ambivalent love-hate relationship. His mother had a good deal of control over his behavior, yet he often abused her emotionally and rebelled against her.
- His personality is distorted. Usually there is a history of being a loner or socially involved only on a superficial level.
- He often accomplishes feats that others are unable to do. Batterers love to impress their women. Generally, they are extremely sensitive to differences in other people's behavior. They can predict reactions to others faster than most. Under stress, their sensitivity becomes paranoid in nature.[2]

COMMON CHARACTERISTICS OF THE WOMAN WHO IS BATTERED

- She has low self-esteem. She typically underestimates her own abilities. She doubts her competence and underplays her successes. She usually doubts her abilities to perform wifely duties. Thus, the man's constant criticism of her affects her judgment.
- She assumes the guilt for the batterer's behavior and believes he would change his behavior if she would

change her own. In truth, she has little or no control over his behavior.

- She believes all the myths about battering relationships.
- She is a traditionalist about the home and strongly believes in family unity and the prescribed feminine sex role stereotype. She is ready to give up her career no matter how important it is to her. She gives the man the right to make the final decisions on how the family income is spent.
- She accepts responsibility for the batterer's actions.
- She suffers from guilt yet denies the terror and anger she feels. She is a keeper of the peace. She attempts to control people and situations in the environment to keep the batterer from losing his temper. She makes herself responsible for creating a safe environment for everyone.
- She presents a passive face to the world but has the strength to manipulate her environment enough to prevent further violence and being killed.
- She has severe stress reactions with psychophysical complaints. Generally, battered women are hard workers who live under constant fear and stress. She is able to withstand enormous amounts of pain during battering, yet often complains about minor ailments such as fatigue, backaches, headaches, restlessness, inability to sleep, depression, anxiety, and suspiciousness.
- She uses sex as a way to establish intimacy.
- She believes that no one will be able to help her resolve her predicament except herself. She may report that this is her first exposure to a violent man. Many of these women describe their fathers as traditionalists who treated them like fragile dolls, which made them believe they couldn't take care of themselves and had to depend on a man.
- She may be overly gullible and trusting of others.[3]

COMMON CHARACTERISTICS OF
CHILDREN IN VIOLENT HOMES

- Children who grow up in violent homes may suffer from loss of sleep (many attacks happen when they are in bed), and they may not be receiving adequate nutrition or nurturing. These losses may contribute to physical, emotional/psychological, and cognitive delays in their development. They may feel helpless in the face of attacks against a parent that they cannot stop or lessen. These feelings of powerlessness often lead to depression.
- Children of domestic violence are found in all socio-economic levels and in all educational, racial, and age-groups.
- They exhibit a combination of limited tolerance, poor impulse control, and martyrlike long-suffering.
- They experience depression, considerable stress and psychosomatic disorders (bodily disorders induced by mental or emotional disturbances), excessive school absenteeism, and have hidden symptoms of characterological dysfunction (withdrawal, low self-esteem, hyperactivity, and so on).
- They are economically and emotionally dependent. They are at high risk for substance abuse, sexual acting out, running away, isolation, loneliness, and fear.
- They have a very shaky definition of self, grappling with the childlike responses of their parents as models.
- They have low self-esteem.
- They experience a mixture of hope and depression—depression that there is no way out. Peer groups, if available, can be their most important contact.
- They may exhibit increased social isolation with their peers.
- They may "bargain" their behavior with their parents, "proving" themselves, as do their mothers.[4]

Men abuse for many reasons, but there is no excuse for abusing or controlling the ones we love. Domestic violence is a crime. There is hope and help for those who are hurting and those who hurt others.

"I truthfully underestimated the seriousness of the violence that was occurring in that home," one pastor lamented. Here's the rest of the lesson that opened his eyes to the realities of domestic violence:

After praying with the wife, I in effect told her to go home and try harder. In the back of my mind I guess I thought she was exaggerating or that her husband had really had a bad day. Perhaps beneath that quiet exterior this woman exercised a gift for making her husband violent. The next time I heard about her, she had been hospitalized because of a severe life-threatening altercation. Her husband had beaten her and pushed her down the second-floor stairs. She was bruised, had sustained several broken ribs, and had a bad concussion and internal bleeding.

These are the moments when you want to turn in your ordination. A sweet woman had come to me for counseling and protection. It had probably been a supreme act of courage in her life. Instead of representing Christ to her, I had allowed all my ignorance and my helplessness, my male prejudice, my own denial, not wanting to think that one of my parishioners would act in such a violent way, to prevent me from extending intervention and healing. I could hardly look that woman in the eye when I called on her in the hospital ward. Believe me—I began to learn all I could about the problem of wife abuse in my community.[5]

Of women experiencing domestic violence, it is estimated that more than 60 percent who reach out for help go to a spiritual leader first. Too many times the spiritual leader sends them back home into submission, not understanding the dynamics of the violent home.

So WHY DO MEN ABUSE?

To better understand the reasons men batter, it is first helpful to consider the expectations society places on men, how these expectations are internalized, and how they manifest themselves in behavior. Biologically, masculine characteristics are readily identifiable and include facial hair, deepening of the voice at puberty, and male genitalia. But masculinity acted out is a learned behavior that generally reflects the prevailing attitudes of the society in which the man lives. Let's consider four categories in the myths of masculinity.

"No Sissy Stuff"

The term "sissy" means being like a sister—a female. It refers to a male who is timid, cowardly, and effeminate. "No sissy stuff" means that it's not acceptable to have feminine qualities or behaviors. Even in this enlightened age, most boys are taught to avoid dolls, girls, and other feminine activities. They are largely directed to play with the things "men" are made of, such as footballs, guns, and superheroes. They are encouraged to avoid crying, to turn off their emotions by keeping them bundled up inside. Vulnerability is seen as an undesirable trait. In order to be accepted at school and in the neighborhood, boys must mask their personalities. In doing so, they deceive themselves as well as the world around them.

"Be the Big Wheel"

Boys and young men are encouraged to be the boss, the quarterback, the driver, the chief executive officer. The "big wheel" has power and runs the show. He's the head of the group, and that group might be the neighborhood gang, the local bowling team, or his own family. The big wheel is the one who makes all the other wheels move, the one in charge. If a man operates under a distorted version of masculinity, he'll find a place to be the big wheel. If he can't be the big wheel at work, then he works harder to be the big wheel at home.

Our society, of course, models this concept. Our country acts as the big wheel to other nations. On a corporate level, men compete for the position to be the biggest wheel. Even in Western movies the fastest gunfighter will eventually be beaten. This sense of competition fosters a sense of mistrust, a feeling of insecurity, a tendency to isolate, and an obligation to stuff feelings inside so they're not seen as weaknesses.

"Be the Sturdy Oak"

"Mighty oaks from little acorns grow," the old saying goes. The sturdy oak is oblivious to stress and strain, unyielding before the storm, impervious to pain—at least on the outside. Men who buy into the myths of masculinity show happiness and rage but ignore the large gray area that separates these two extremes. Professional sports players are seen as the sturdiest of society's oaks. They shake off pain as though it doesn't exist, shun intimidation by being more intimidating, and become heroes of violence. Traditional masculinity limits emotions such as fear, pain, nervousness, insecurity, jealousy, and sadness—to be turned to anger, rage, and violence.

"Make Her Life Miserable"

When a woman has had her head kicked in a few times, has suffered the silent treatment for days, or has been called enough disparaging names by her partner, she learns that no matter what the personal cost, it's important to try to keep him happy. The man who operates under the masculine myth wants to assume his place in the pecking order of society. If the boss is getting on his case, he may seek recourse but at least temporarily accepts his boss's authority. When he gets home, however, he takes out his anger and frustration on the woman in his life. In his mind, this is retribution against his boss for making him miserable. He then feels better, because one way or another he's made someone else miserable.

Men who wish to change their behavior need to move away from the traditional model in which anger is the primary feeling. To the traditional man, conflict usually means feelings are denied. As a man starts to change, he begins to see that there are many ways to resolve conflict. He learns that feelings are confusing but can be identified. The new man knows that conflicts can be resolved and that feelings have names. He recognizes that anger is a reaction to a feeling that can be dealt with.

Tension Building

Violence happens in cycles. The tension-building stage comes first, then an explosion. After the adrenaline has dissipated, the man comes back down and goes into what's called the "honeymoon stage." He knows that he has broken the covenant of marriage by the abuse.

A woman who is battered must come to understand that she doesn't need to take another beating in order to have the power to leave. She must understand that the tension-building stage is the time to get out—before the battering occurs. She knows by becoming aware of his behaviors that the escalation stage is going to happen. In Figure 2 we see the difference between a man's and a woman's ability to perceive anger. We're not dealing with her anger at this point but how she responds and what she sees. There may be a period of time in which the couple has been getting along, as we see in the parallel lines of Figure 2. Then something may trigger him, and she sees his anger escalating. Underneath, many things are happening to his body. These are the signs or behaviors she may see:

a. flushed face

b. verbal aggression or innuendoes

c. change in body language

d. noticeable tension

He doesn't recognize his anger until he reacts outwardly, such as by physically abusing, hitting a wall, screaming, yelling, or cursing. Many times he doesn't even think of these things as an explosion of anger—just an expression.

Women need to understand that the escalation has some dynamics in it that she has the ability to recognize. If she has ever been battered, it's a trauma to her mind. She'll subconsciously pick up the pattern, especially over a period of time.

FIGURE 2

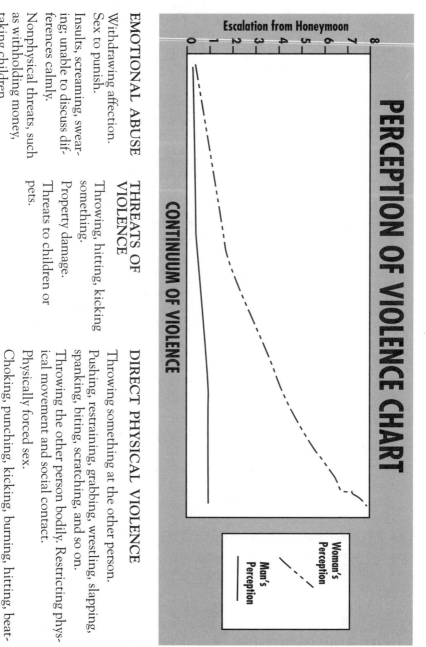

PERCEPTION OF VIOLENCE CHART

Escalation from Honeymoon

8 7 6 5 4 3 2 1 0

Woman's Perception

Man's Perception

CONTINUUM OF VIOLENCE

EMOTIONAL ABUSE

Withdrawing affection.
Sex to punish.
Insults, screaming, swearing; unable to discuss differences calmly.
Nonphysical threats, such as witholding money, taking children.
Interrupting sleep.

THREATS OF VIOLENCE

Throwing, hitting, kicking something.
Property damage.
Threats to children or pets.

DIRECT PHYSICAL VIOLENCE

Throwing something at the other person.
Pushing, restraining, grabbing, wrestling, slapping, spanking, biting, scratching, and so on.
Throwing the other person bodily. Restricting physical movement and social contact.
Physically forced sex.
Choking, punching, kicking, burning, hitting, beating, threatening with weapons or even using them.

Let's look at this pattern. A woman may get along for a period with her partner. Then something will trigger him, maybe at work. It could happen as in the following scenario.

As you hear him pull into the driveway, you get butterflies in your stomach. You don't know exactly why, but as he walks into the house you feel anxious. You don't understand the process, so you ask yourself, *Now what have I done?*

You may not be conscious of the roll of the tire when he turns into the driveway, but your mind is capable of absorbing such small things and realizing when things are not consistent with his normal pattern. Usually when he drives in he doesn't create a special noise. But perhaps on the day he gets triggered, he comes into the driveway a little faster, causing the tires to squeal. He may do this for three or four days in a row. The cycle has begun, and his tension is escalating.

Before long he'll drive in and you'll hear the squeal of the tires—but this time he slams the car door shut quite forcefully. Your subconscious knows the sound of a normal slam of the car door, but this one is different. Two or three days later he comes into the driveway and you hear the squeal of the tires, a little chirp when he hits the brakes, and the slam of the car door. You may not consciously recognize this, but your subconscious has picked it up, and the butterflies in your stomach are now more evident.

This goes on for maybe two or three weeks. Then one day he comes to the back door, and instead of blocking the door with his hand to soften its closing, as he usually does, you hear a loud slam. Two or three days later he walks in, slams the door, and instead of acknowledging you as he generally does, he brushes right past you.

A week later he's so curt that you say to him, "Honey, is everything OK?"

He barks back, "If there were something wrong, you'd know it!"

You try to restore peace, but he sees your communication as provocation. He goes into a blame mode, and you know that it's beyond resolution. You know deep inside that you're going to be battered. For the period of time between the beginning of this pattern and the actual abuse you go into a mode of trying to be extra nice. But you feel rejection. You try cooking his favorite meals. You say to the children, "Kids, hurry up and get your toys picked up—Daddy's home." The kids run to their rooms. You're doing everything you can to create peace. You think you need to take responsibility to try to avoid the battering incident that you know is going to happen.

The longer they're together with continued episodes of battering, the shorter the period of time between the battering incidents.

This stage of escalating tension is where you can see the pattern developing, and this is where those who are being battered should get out. Make a safety plan. Don't wait until the anger has become intensified to run. If you can understand and recognize the patterns of the escalation, go to a safe place—then you can call him and say, "I'm not going to be battered again. You're going to have to get some help, or I'm not coming home."

Explosion

After the escalation stage, we move to the acute battering stage. After he gets past the beginning of the escalation stage and it's moving toward the explosion, it can progress quickly. When he finally goes off, the woman knows it's been coming for weeks. The fear and anxiety is something she lives with internally, knowing it's going to happen and that there's no way to control or avoid it. There's no way to escape from the fear that he has already created by previous abuse.

When he explodes, he "spikes" (see Figure 3) and goes into what we call the "irrational infantile belief system," which usually last for 8 to 10 minutes. He loses touch with reality, but he knows what he's doing. He is in control of his emotions and his Jekyll-and-Hyde personality. When he spikes, he does the depth of his damage. He could kill her during this stage. He can tear up the house and batter her. The longer they're together with continued episodes of battering, the shorter the period of time between the battering incidents. She may call 911. If the police walk into the home at the height of the spike, an officer can get killed, because the batterer is in an irrational, infantile belief system that says, "She's mine, and you have no right to be here." The officer has invaded the batterer's castle in the batterer's sick, patriarchal belief system.

In the Jekyll-and-Hyde syndrome a man has total control of each personality and uses one or the other to maintain power and control over the situation or his partner.

Jan's husband was a top executive for one of the largest corporations in their city. She told her counselors about the degree of abuse and battering she tolerated from her husband. But they knew him—or at least thought they knew him—and would say things like "He wouldn't do something like that." Yet one time he came home at 3 A.M. after having an affair and got Jan out of bed to beat her. She ran about one-third of a mile into a field where she tripped and fell into a freshly plowed furrow. As she fell down, a foot came down onto the back of her head and drove her face into the ground. She felt the double-barrel 12-gauge on the back of her head, just behind her ear, and heard and felt the cock of the gun as he pulled both hammers back.

This is the typical Jekyll-and-Hyde abusive personality. It is a controlling, undeveloped type of personality with no character. It is capable of killing, capable of assault and battery, capable of manipulation, capable of all kinds of abuse. The world, however, sees the pseudo or false personality of the nice guy. The woman's friends and even the coworkers of her husband usually doubt that he is a batterer and might even think she is the one who's crazy.

In the Jekyll-and-Hyde syndrome a man has total control of each personality and uses one or the other to maintain power and control over the situation or his partner. She lives

FIGURE 3

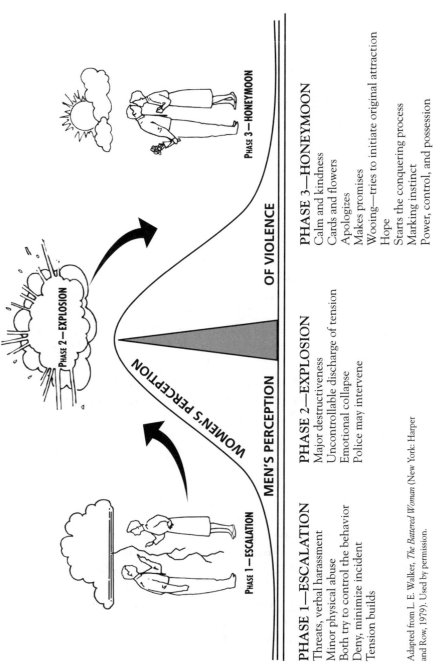

PHASE 1—ESCALATION
PHASE 2—EXPLOSION
PHASE 3—HONEYMOON

WOMEN'S PERCEPTION

MEN'S PERCEPTION   OF VIOLENCE

PHASE 1—ESCALATION
Threats, verbal harassment
Minor physical abuse
Both try to control the behavior
Deny, minimize incident
Tension builds

PHASE 2—EXPLOSION
Major destructiveness
Uncontrollable discharge of tension
Emotional collapse
Police may intervene

PHASE 3—HONEYMOON
Calm and kindness
Cards and flowers
Apologizes
Makes promises
Wooing—tries to initiate original attraction
Hope
Starts the conquering process
Marking instinct
Power, control, and possession

Adapted from L. E. Walker, *The Battered Woman* (New York: Harper
and Row, 1979). Used by permission.

in fear because he is so volatile. But after he de-escalates following the spike and the adrenaline has dissipated, he comes right back down and goes into the bathroom, combs his hair, shaves quickly, maybe changes his shirt and slacks, and might even meet the responding police officers at the door. If so, he would greet them and say something like "Guys, come on in. It's been a rough night. Boy, I'm glad you're here." He's coherent and overcooperative as they walk into the kitchen, where they find the woman huddled on the floor up against a cabinet. With her hair in the air, mascara running, a bloody nose, a ripped blouse, broken ribs, and knees drawn up to her chest, she sobs amid the torn-up kitchen with chairs turned over and food on the walls. He's cool, calm, and collected, and she looks like a mental case.

When a woman is being battered, the batterer pushes her to the emotional and mental level of a three- to five-year-old while he's in a seven- to nine-year-old emotional and mental state of a playground bully. If the arriving officers walk over and say, "Ma'am, can you talk about this?" she can't get a word out. "Do you want us to take you to a shelter?" She's afraid to go to a shelter. She's afraid to talk. She's afraid of the consequence of even leaving him because of the power and control she has been experiencing throughout their relationship.

Honeymoon Stage

As soon as the officers leave, if they don't take the batterer in, or if law enforcement is never called, he goes into the honeymoon stage. The Bible tells us that the husband should be willing to die for the wife (Eph. 5:25). He is to cherish her. He is to honor her as his own body. But when a man batters his wife, he has broken that covenant. She knows it, and he knows it. He realizes that he's treading on thin ice.

The first thing he wants to do is go to the bedroom to make up. But domestic violence is not foreplay. What kind of man thinks a woman who is bleeding, sobbing, and crying with broken ribs, smeared lipstick, and mascara running down her cheeks would want to make love? Still, the first thing the abuser wants to do is to make love to her—but it isn't really making love. It's not even a sex act. It's a possession act, and it is abuse.

When we disobey God's principles, we end up like brute beasts, working off of instinctual responses (Jude 10). When a man has battered his partner, he knows that he has broken covenant, and the first thing that he must do is to bring her back into covenant. To a man, sex is covenant. When we have broken covenant in a marriage relationship by battering, the intense, instinctual drive of the animal instinct of the fallen nature of man wants to mark her, because the moment he marks her by sex, he owns her again. In his sick way, he thinks he has restored covenant. But for the woman it's the emptiest feeling she can feel.

This is not about love. It's not even about sex. It's not about relationship. It's about ownership. When he has reconquered her, the cycle starts again.

Until he becomes accountable and responsible for his behavior and starts getting help in developing his character and his core, the abuse will not stop.

If she says to him, "You'll never make love to me again until you get help and this cycle stops," he'll start a wooing process. He might buy flowers or offer to take her out to eat; he may promise to go to church and to get counseling; he'll probably want to remodel the house and buy some new furniture. Some men want to buy another house and start all over again. But if we don't deal with the central issues, it's going to happen again, because we can't change on our own.

When the man goes into the honeymoon stage, his wife gets to see for a period of time a window of the good man she saw at first and fell in love with. The problem is that the good man is a pseudo good man. It's not the real inside of the man. A man who batters has a sick core. His core and character are undeveloped, and the dark side is dominant. Until he becomes accountable and responsible for his behavior and starts getting help in developing his character and his core, the abuse will not stop. That's the only hope we have. But without proper intervention, he has no ability to make a lasting change. So the excuses keep coming. The promises are broken. The cycle of violence continues. She sees his remorse. She hears his promises. Somewhere deep inside, she catches a glimpse of the guy she fell in love with. She hopes against hope that this time he'll change.

Chapter 5

DRIVEN BY THE WOUNDS

The wounds of childhood affect us for a lifetime. Psychologists call this phenomenon fixation. Simply put, fixation involves the arrest of emotional development at the point of trauma. The trauma can be ongoing (such as rejection throughout one's childhood), a cluster of two or three events in a short time period (such as the death of both parents in a short timeframe), or one major devastating event (such as rape, molestation, or other physical abuse).

There are four broad categories of trauma that most commonly arrest the development of the child: rejection, sexual abuse (incest or molestation), emotional abuse, and physical abuse. Any one of these or a cluster of them can freeze the development of the child and cause him or her to shut down emotionally. The pain is simply too great for one so young to handle. The child does not have the ability to see the reality of the situation that causes the trauma. Instead, he or she assumes responsibility for the deviant behavior of the adult and thinks, *What did I do to cause him [or her] to do that to me?*

Paul writes to the Corinthian church, "When I was a child, I talked like a child, I thought like a child, I reasoned like a child; now that I have become a man, I am done with childish ways and have put them aside" (1 Cor. 13:11, AMP.).

How does a child's thinking and reasoning differ from that of an adult? Research shows that the child under the age of puberty is lacking the chemicals in the brain to think in abstract terms and see the whole picture. A child is focused on one thing at any given time. He or she thinks in concrete terms.[1]

A little boy who is chasing a ball that bounces into the street is focused on retrieving the ball. But his father sees the truck coming, gauges the speed of the truck, screams at his son, runs to rescue him, and saves his life—even if the ball is run over by the truck. The father sees the entire picture. The child sees only the ball. By nature, he thinks only about now. Children are self-centered, me-oriented, and they demand instant gratification. Yet they need boundaries and consequences to learn obedience to authority and consequences for disobedience. They need structure and rules. If a child is wounded by rejection, sexual abuse, emotional abuse, or physical abuse, the emotional growth is locked up out of the child's fear of being damaged and not worthy of love. The child loses his or her self-worth and feels flawed and powerless.

How the Child Develops

Jewish custom recognizes three major stages of human life (see figure 4). The first is the age of directives, from birth to age 12. Prov. 22:6 says, "Train up a child in the way he should go: and when he is old, he will not depart from it" (KJV). At this stage, dependence upon the family unit is dominant.

At age 13 the Jewish boy has his bar mitzvah. This rite of passage signifies the transition from childhood to adulthood. At this stage of accountability the child officially enters the age of decision. The rabbi says to the boy who is preparing for his bar mitzvah, "Now you have reached the age of accountability. You are responsible for the results of your behaviors. You are accountable for what you do. There are going to be consequences for your decisions in life, and you are responsible for those consequences. You are becoming an adult. You will be out in the world making decisions and being responsible for them. Today we release your parents of the liability for your behavior."

In Jewish tradition a man is not considered a mature man, although he may be married, until he is 30 years of age. It was at this age that Jesus came into His fullness of ministry. But

FIGURE 4

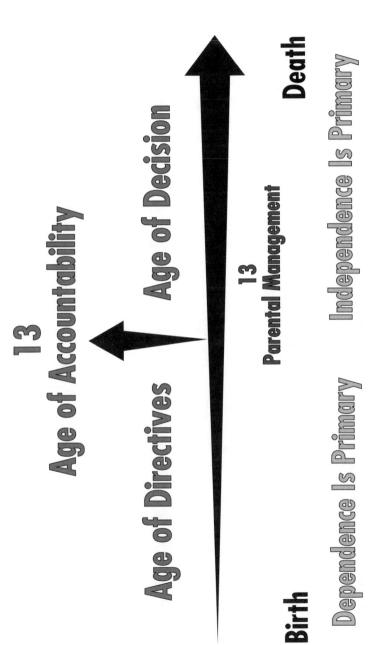

up to that point, from age 13 to 30, is what is called the age of parental management. In our Western tradition we don't have 17 years of parental management of our children; it's more like 5 years. One of the reasons the Jewish race has been so phenomenal in the areas of business and financial success is that their males have 17 years of training in making decisions and following in the path of the previous males of the family. They're getting a reality check and learning to be submissive to wise counsel, as the Bible so clearly stresses.

As earlier stated, the individual enters the age of decision at age 13. We continue at this stage until death. As we grow older, we become more confident in our decisions. We can find options. We can move forward. We can be successful. The normal 13-, 14-, and 15-year-old child is moving out of the age of directives into the age of decision.

This age-old Jewish tradition of these three stages of life parallels the findings of modern psychological research. One widely accepted view of child development is that of Eric Erickson. Erickson identified eight stages of development in a person's life, but the first six (see Figure 5) are those that apply to the areas we are concentrating on.

PUTTING IT TOGETHER

If emotional growth has been arrested, inner character will not develop normally.

How do the traumas of childhood drive our behavior? The wounds that never healed force us to resort to our survival instinct. Preservation at all costs—that's our drive to stay alive. But children don't have the ability or know-how to change their circumstances. So in most situations they learn to cope with the garbage. A superficial mask sometimes hides the pain, but not without cost.

If emotional growth has been arrested, inner character will not develop normally. Instead, a child can create a pseudopersonality that becomes a mask to protect from rejection. In this process the child is trying to meet the expectations from the people who are important in life, but in the process his or her own development is sacrificed. Crucial areas of relationships and personal life management are hindered.

Anger Management

It takes an adult with decision-making abilities to manage anger and recognize that rage must have a source. You can't make me, as an adult, angry unless I allow you to make me angry. I can choose not to allow you to manipulate me and make me angry. However, it's easier to make a child angry, because children have no decision-making abilities.

Have you ever dealt with a person who is very unpredictable and short-tempered? Probably he or she was wounded as a child. Because of this person's childish behavior and lack of ability to manage anger, it seems that others always pick on him or her. This person wonders what's wrong and always feels like a child on the inside. He or she feels as if everybody in the world has control over his or her emotions. If we're arrested in our development, anger management is not one of our skills.

Cooperation

If I'm arrested in my development, I fail to work as a team member. I should be a confident decision-maker, but since I'm arrested in development, I try to sway everyone my way. If I don't get my way, I pout and withdraw. If I'm outvoted in a church board meeting, then I withdraw, resign, or talk behind the other board members' backs to make sure my opinion is heard. The same thing is true on the job. If we are arrested in development, we don't understand that we have to work as a team. Cooperation in the home, on the job, and in spiritual life seems out of the question.

Conflict Resolution

Conflict resolution is not a part of the equation in a person with arrested development. Men especially are good at this. If a man can't resolve the conflict, he just walks around

FIGURE 5

ERIK ERICKSON'S SIX LIFE STAGES*

Stage	Age (Approx.)	Task	Aspects of Tasks	If Not Accomplished	Lasting Accomplishment of Successful Outcome
I	Infancy (birth to 1 yr.)	*Basic trust*	*Physical and emotional* "mothering." A sense of order and stability in the events he or she experiences; feelings of being wanted, loved, and cared for.	*Basic Mistrust.* Life remains chaotic, unconnected. Child is sickly, physically and psychologically disabled. High infant mortality; childhood autism; academic retardation.	*Drive and Hope*
II	Toddler Age (1 to 3 yr.)	*Autonomy*	Learns to stand on own two feet; feeds self, and so on. Controls bodily functions. Makes basic needs known through language. Discovers choices; learns to say "no" and "yes." Accepts "no" as well as "yes." Learns the rules of society; "may and may not do."	*Shame and Doubt.* Lack of autonomy produces passive dependence on others; unable to assert own will results in overobedience; unable to accept "no" results in personality constantly rebellious; perhaps "delinquent."	*Self-Control and Will Power*
III	Preschool Age (about 4 to 6 yr.)	*Initiative*	Learns geography and time, can go and come back, can think in terms of future, has developed memory, learns beginning adult roles. More loving, cooperative, secure in family. Good chance of becoming a "moral" person.	*Guilt.* Wants always to be in control. Sense of competition drives person to be "overcompetitive"; may be always outside law.	*Direction and Purpose*
IV	School Age (about 6 to 12 yr.)	*Industry*	Learning the "how tos" of society; in Western society masters "3 Rs"; begins to understand matrices of society. Learns to feel worthy and competent.	*Inferiority.* If person fails to learn industry, begins to feel inferior compared to others. If overlearns industry, may become too "task oriented" and overconforms to society.	*Method and Competence*
V	Adolescence (12 to late teens or early adulthood)	*Identity*	Sexual maturation and sexual identity. Discovers role in life; ponders question "Who am I?" as distinct from family. Develops social friendships; rejects family.	*Role Confusion.* May not achieve a personal identity separate from family. May not become socially adult or sexually stable.	*Devotion and Fidelity*
VI	Early Adulthood	*Intimacy*	Learns to share passions, interests, problems with another individual. Learns to think of "we," "our," "us" instead of "I," "my," or "me." Affiliates with others; family, place of work, community. Achieves stability.	*Isolation.* Inability to be intimate with others. Becomes fixated at adolescent level of sensation seeking and self-pleasure. Avoids responsibility. Lacks "roots" and stability.	*Affiliation and Love*

*The first six stages of Erickson's eight stages are dealt with here.
Adapted from Erik H. Erickson, *Identity and the Life Cycle* (New York and London: W. W. Norton and Co., 1980).

with a whole bunch of conflicts unresolved behind him. It doesn't bother him that much. Women are different. They want resolution at the time of the conflict. If they have something unresolved in their lives, they want to solve it. Women want closure. Men don't need closure. If a child has a conflict, falls down, and gets wounded, where does he or she go? Mommy or Daddy will fix it. But when we're dealing with arrested development, we find that a man will run into a problem and then want his wife to fix it. She'll run into a problem as a victim and want him to fix it. That's what draws the couple together in their dysfunction, the commonness of the need rather than the commonness of choice.

Goal Orientation

It's common for a battered victim to say, "You know, he's a good man. He has a lot of great ideas, but he's the biggest con man and the biggest liar I've ever met." When we're arrested in development, we set high goals. In fact, we set impossible goals and get angry with ourselves for setting them, with no hope of ever achieving them.

For instance, when the man sets the goal, he tells his wife what he's going to do. He gets his strokes up front. However, he doesn't reach any of his goals. After about six months of this, he comes up with a new set of goals. When he talks them over with his wife, she wants to say, "You're the biggest liar I've ever met," but she's afraid of getting hit. She can usually produce a list of the things he's said he would do but never followed through on. Finally, she looks at him as a blowhard and a liar.

When a man says, "I'm going to do this," in his mind he has already done it. If he's arrested in development, he gets his glory from saying, "I'm going to do it." Then he starts projects and doesn't finish them. He has a lot of open-ended stuff ahead of him and a lot of open-ended stuff behind him.

Let me add a piece to this equation that may hurt a little. What about a daughter whose father says, "Tonight it's just going to be you and me. We're going to go out and do something, and no one else gets to go." But Daddy doesn't show up. She waits up until she can't keep her eyes open any longer, still hoping he'll be home and they'll do what he promised. She finally falls asleep, and Mommy comes and tucks her into bed. In the morning when she wakes up, tears run down her cheeks. Her daddy disappointed her. Then she marries a man like Daddy, because she's familiar with that type of personality. Her husband repeatedly disappoints her. Then people wonder why she doesn't trust men. She was wounded by a father who said great things about what he was going to do but didn't do them. She gets an instant replay in a husband who has a lot of great ideas and goals. Finally she says, "I'll never do this again."

Emotional Intimacy

If we're arrested in development, emotional intimacy is totally foreign. Under the age of puberty a child is basically asexual. We find that if a child has been molested and/or sexually abused in a cluster of events or a long-term situation, the child is stuck in a diffused sexuality. If we're wounded sexually, emotionally, or physically as a child, marriage—especially for men—is about sex, and the emotional component is more like a mother type of thing. "I want a wife—I don't want a mother," he says. He will need a tremendous amount of sexual attention in an attempt to fulfill his needs but does not realize that as an adult there is emotional intimacy tied to sexual intimacy.

Financial Management and Accountability

If we're arrested in development, we find that much of the time we're financial disasters. We get tied up on material things because we're not happy with life. We know something is wrong, so we spend, spend, spend. We run the credit cards to the limit. Eventually we're in financial disaster. In some cases, we avoid working on our own recovery program because we can't see it as something tangible. The childish priority is self-gratification in financial matters, again wanting what we want when we want it. We want to buy something tangible. We don't want to invest in our own recovery, something we can't see.

During my first marriage to Judy, she would say to me, "How much money do we have in the bank? I need to get some groceries."

I would say, "What's it to you? You don't need to know what's in the bank."

It's normal between a husband and wife that both know everything about the finances. Both should know what the debt load is. If both of you are working and pool your money, you both know where it's going and how much you have at any given time. In financial matters both great and small, there are items that both marriage partners should understand. They both should have access to the finances and talk about spending issues. But for those arrested in development, it feels as if somebody is asking a question that's none of his or her business. Judy had every right to know what was in the checking account to go buy groceries, but because of my arrested development, I wanted nothing to do with accountability. In my mind, Judy had become a mother, an authority, and I resented it and resisted it. I thought that since I was the head of this family, it was my money.

This area is important in premarital counseling because it seems to be one of the toughest areas for couples to deal with. If there is arrest in the development, he wants control of the money and she's along for the ride. Accountability feels like authority, and in arrested development authority is resisted.

Sexual Development and Intimacy

Sexual development in a person with a childlike mind-set is self-centered. Such a man is not interested in foreplay, communication, or bonding. It's a real effort for him to take the time with his mate to talk about things that are very serious. His relationships will be very superficial. He'll talk about things that are not deep. He won't talk about resolution of conflict. He won't bond. It's just easier in the developmental structure of arrested development to take care of his own

FIGURE 6

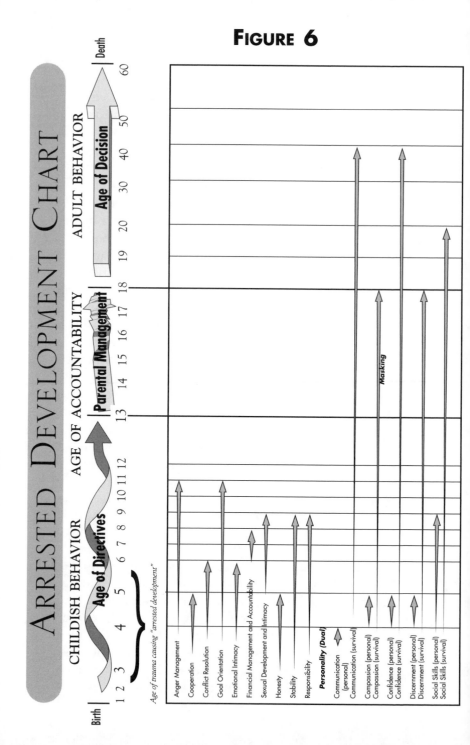

needs. The more that happens, the less the need for his partner. She becomes a person to be owned but not to be nurtured and cared for.

Adult masturbation could be a carryover of arrested development in childhood because such a person has never developed the skills and maturity to relate in an adult-to-adult relationship. Responsible adult sexual relationships require commitment and emotional responsibility, accountability, and acknowledgment of each other. It requires communication of feelings and valuing the other person to reach toward an ongoing growth pattern between a husband and wife. Masturbation is an easy way out, not requiring any of these things.

Honesty

When we try to look mature but we aren't, we become manipulative. We embellish, we stretch the truth, and we lie to survive. "Why would I be honest with you and expose my childishness?" is the unspoken question of such persons. "I'm going to cover it up. I'm a pseudomature adult. In fact, I have answers to questions you'll never ask. I can run your life. I can plot your life. I can tell you what to do because I think I'm more mature than you are."

It's interesting that in the area of honesty we'll do what we have to do to maintain this façade of a pseudoadult, a mature-looking personality. However, our behavior and actions speak louder than words. We get found out almost every time. It's just uncanny how it all comes to the surface. Soon people will say, "Well, you can't trust or believe him [her] for anything. Don't even bother." That's a sign of arrested development.

Stability

When we're arrested in development, we have developed a "dual personality" that lacks stability. James 1:8 says, "A double minded man is unstable in all his ways" (KJV). Double-mindedness can certainly be interpreted as the instability of a person who is aging chronologically but is childish in his or her ways. There is no stability whatsoever. It's a chameleonic syndrome that says, "Wherever I am, I'll adjust my personality to the situation." Thus, there is less fear of rejection. Such a person has no confidence in a belief system, no stability in a Christian experience, no stability financially, no stability in the home, and no stability on the job. It is an ebb and flow of whatever is going on—ride with the tide and go with the flow.

Responsibility

Responsibility is a learned character trait that's taught by example. The problem so many times is that we have children in this day and age who are raising children; that is, parents who have been arrested in development and are now raising their own children.

In their later years parents who were arrested in development become really helpless. They want their married children to take care of them and make decisions for them. The roles reverse, and the elderly become childish as they try to make the children finish the growth pattern that never happened in their own family of origin. Yet the developmental arrest of the child also resists responsibility, so the cycle gets passed on year after year and generation after generation. The child will not be more mature than the parents of the family of origin unless someone steps in to help him or her mature.

Communication

The dual personality is obvious in the communication that takes place within the home of someone with arrested development. A husband and wife in this situation can talk about the weather, the house, a vacation, the children, the car, the neighbors, and their extended families. However, they cannot or will not talk to each other about deep things such as feelings, needs, or relationship issues, because these may reveal who they really are, and that would lead to rejection and pain they can't handle. They're living a façade. There's no resolution of conflict, emotional bonding, or growth as a couple. There's no depth of working and building a relationship. They are frozen, and the relationship is frozen too.

Compassion

In the home and personal life of those arrested in their development, compassion is lacking. The wife can get sick, and her husband doesn't give a rip. His attitude is "You have to schedule your sickness, because I need the laundry done, and you're going to have to get up and cook the meals and have sex." He has no compassion for his wife when she's sick. Let him get sick, however, and life stops to wait on him. She sees the worst side of him. Yet the world thinks he's wonderful: somebody's in financial trouble, and he'll give whatever he has to help, but she's at home with the utilities shut off; she has no groceries, but he's out with his buddies and their wives picking up the tab. He might look very compassionate and mature to the outside world, but she sees that he doesn't even have compassion for his own children.

Confidence

Out in the world the man wears a mask and looks like the most confident person in the world. If the woman ever shared that she's battered or emotionally abused, people would say, "Something's wrong with her. We know him. We've known him for years. He's not that kind of person. What are you trying to do—destroy him?" Yet inside the home he's a mess. He has no confidence. He has the "poor me" syndrome. He plays the martyr; he sets it up that way so that she will nurture and take care of him. He doesn't want a mother figure who would trigger his resistance to authority, but he wants someone to take care of him, pick up after him, and resolve his problems; yet he resents being told what to do.

Discernment

The man's personal discernment is way off. This guy is in full-tilt denial, but he could tell you exactly what he thinks is wrong with your life. He's living it so he knows what you're going through. He has the answers for everyone else, but none for himself.

Social Skills

This man might be able to go to France and order off the menu and have all the social skills in the world. But in his own home he sits around in his underwear watching television, belching, passing gas, and setting poor examples for the kids. He can go to church or be on the job, and everyone is impressed; however, the duality is most evident in the home. The arrested development is his way of life.

Moving emotionally from the age of directives to the age of decision is not only for Jewish children. If I view life as a child and feel that my decisions are dictated by my indecision, my circumstance, or someone who controls me, then inwardly I feel powerless over myself and my life. As a result, I determine to control everything around me, including people and situations. Like it or not, I'm driven by my wounds.

Chapter 6

THE REACTIVE LIFESTYLE

As we have seen, if a child experiences any one of or a cluster of the following wounds, it can be debilitating to his or her development. Let's examine these more closely:

REJECTION

Rejection is one of the toughest things for a human being to handle. It is worse than terminal cancer. At least a person with terminal cancer knows there will be an end and can prepare for what is ahead. Death is closure, and we can usually handle that in our minds; we're programmed to do so.

Rejection, however, is open-ended. In our minds, it lasts forever. There's no closure to it. We can trace the intense fear of rejection to our childhood—something that happened to us; the traumas; things our parents, peer groups, brothers and sisters told us. Rejection can happen at conception and it can include abandonment, a critical spirit, perfectionism, putdowns, neglect, and so on. All of the following wounds fall under the umbrella of rejection.

Incest and Molestation

Sexual abuse rejects my privacy, my body, my value, and my esteem. It causes me to feel invalidated from the human race.

> Incest = sexual abuse between family members
> Molestation = sexual abuse outside of family

Emotional Abuse

Emotional abuse is any communication, admonition, or reproof that does not uplift, edify, or bring conflict resolution. Emotional abuse creates a blueprint for life in the mind of the child. We call them "life commandments." Examples: "You're stupid." "I wish you were never born!" "Who do you think you are?" "Shut up! Who asked you?" "Can't you do anything right?" "Quit crying or I'll give you something to cry about."

Physical Abuse

Physical abuse is any touch not given in love, respect, and dignity. It also emotionally degrades and steals the value system and creates fear.

When the abuses described above occur, they produce the following reactions in a child's life.

Loss of Self-respect

No matter what happens to me, my value as a person does not diminish. When I'm wounded, though, I cannot find or feel this worth. The most obvious result is a loss of self-respect. This will manifest itself in many ways. I will

1. lose my sense of security
2. not develop an ability to trust
3. doubt truth
4. fear knowledge

As we look at the roots of our reactions, the "reactive lifestyle," there are five categories we must understand: rejection and the four manifested wounds of incest, molestation, emotional abuse, and physical abuse. Any one of these or any cluster of these will arrest the development of the child. Rejection in the original family will stunt the developmental structure of the child. If we add some emotional abuse or physical abuse, the child's development will be stunted. We'll work for years trying to find an answer.

If incest, molestation, emotional abuse, or physical abuse happens in the prepuberty child, the child immediately loses his or her self-esteem. The child has an inherent value from his or her Creator at birth. That value is his or her security to face the world and is translated into security for the child, which reads like this: "I am worthy of somebody loving me." The child can then receive the love of his or her parents, because he or she has self-esteem and value. Self-esteem, therefore, is security. When that security is broken by somebody doing something in any one or a combination of those arenas, the child immediately loses self-esteem. The child immediately has no security, so he or she must become self-secure: *My world is not safe. My boundaries have been violated. I must not be worthy of respect and dignity. I cannot trust even my parents to be there for me. I have no security, so I must be my own security.* The child then begins to doubt truth. The child will not receive truth from anyone and starts to develop his or her own truth and develops his or her own feelings, which become truth for the child. We think that our truth (which is really a lie) is dependable, because we doubt anyone else's truth.

Fear of Knowledge

The next thing that happens is fear of knowledge. The child doesn't want to know what's going on. We see people who have symptoms of disease but are afraid to go to the doctor. They're afraid of the truth. They're afraid of knowledge. When the disease progresses and they finally go to the doctor, it's too late—the disease is diagnosed as terminal. Why does it turn out this way? Because we doubt knowledge and fear the truth. We live our adult life, therefore, in denial. We don't want to hear the truth.

Fear of Rejection

The next thing that happens is that out of our fear we move into an area of rejection in our lives. The fear of rejection may cause us to expend a lot of energy trying to keep from being rejected. If I fear rejection, how do I deal with it? I reject myself first. I diffuse the situation so you cannot hurt me. If I have rejected myself, I cannot accept you, so I will reject you too. I will not allow you into my world. We will be surface friends, but when you want to become a close friend, I'll blow you away. I have no ability to trust or receive. I destroy myself, and in destroying myself I destroy others and kill the ability for relationships. This brings isolation.

Isolation

I can't live isolated like that. Therefore, I have to have a self-protection plan. It is this: if you get too close to me, I'll lash out at you. I'll drive you away. I'll pull up an instantaneous fence that comes right out of the ground and hide behind that. I'll keep you away from me at any cost. I just know that if you know me you won't like me. How do I keep you away from me? I lash out. I talk behind your back. I destroy you. I become critical. I become unforgiving. I become inflexible. I set a standard for you that I couldn't meet. When you don't meet it, I lash out and become your judge, jury, and executioner. Now I can't always lash out at the drop of a hat when the need to protect myself arises unless I have a reservoir of bitterness.

Therefore, I collect and categorize injustices of my life. I will not forgive. I will not let go. I can remember every word you said, and I have that tucked into my reservoir. With the reservoir fired up, I can fire off at the drop of a hat. I can curtly put you in your place and keep you out of my life. I couldn't do that without having a reservoir that's always burning to protect myself from your getting to know me. It hurts to live that way, so now what I do is cover up that layer and go into full-tilt denial. I stuff my feelings. I freeze my feelings. I choose not to get in touch with my feelings. I justify my behaviors.

Now I'm set up for life. I know I'm no good. I know I'm going to be rejected, so I'll reject you first. If you get too close to me, I've got enough bitterness to lash out and totally destroy you.

Have you ever met people with a sense of humor that will cut you to the heart? When it starts happening in a marriage relationship it's devastating, because then we hurt the one we love the most. I have my protection system set up, but nothing's wrong with me. I'm fine. It's the whole world that's out of step. Something is wrong with you. If you would just ask me, I could tell you what's wrong with you.

Childhood Wounds

A child who has been rejected by molestation or abuse is easily intimidated. I have dealt with women who say in effect, "Do I have a sign on my forehead that says 'Victim—Abuse Me'? Why don't I have the ability to resist? Why can't I ever set boundaries? Why do I allow others to step over my boundaries?" This happens because of our early childhood wounds —we're easily intimidated. A child is easily intimidated, and as adults we carry this trait into our adult lifestyle. It's based on the fear of rejection.

As the other reactions take root in our lives, our denial system is firmly in place. The results are that we stuff our reactions, denying our emotions and repressing our memories. We're numb. The effects of the wounds are easy to spot, whether in childhood, the teen years, or adulthood. They show up in our jobs, our marriages, our friendships, and our spiritual lives. As wounded children we're easily intimidated.

The child starts escalating in rebellion because he or she feels, *No one knows what happened to me, but I know I'm no good. I know I'm different. I know I'm not ever going to be right again and I'm not lovable, so I'm going to act up just to see if my folks can still love me.* The child begins to act up and causes the parents to question, "What's going on here? We've treated our child lovingly. He's been responsive, and all of a sudden he's acting up with rebellion and an almost hateful attitude." The more the parent loves, the more the child acts up. There's never a finish line for either the parents or the child until they deal with the issue. There is a restlessness and a lack of attention with the child. The self-doubt causes him or her to be somewhat hyperactive or withdrawn. In the self-protection area are a refining of disobedience and an open rebellion. Hostility arises. The child is becoming quite aggressive, with exaggerating, lying, and what we call "blame shifting."

For example, my mom and I are at home, and I'm the only child in the family. Dad has been out of town for a week on business, and Mom finds the cookie jar open. "It's empty," Mom says. "Who ate the cookies?" With cookie crumbs all over my face and on my shirt, I quickly blurt out, "Not me!" The blame shift of the child is obvious: failing to connect the question, the answer, and the evidence. These three items logically connect, but the child doesn't connect them.

As wounded teens we now find that there is a false front that is quite well developed. I use the illustration of myself. I was an angry teen in junior high school. It was during that time that I was being molested by a teacher's aid. The teenagers I went to school with, whose parents came to my father's church, told my mother, "Something's wrong with your son, Paul. He professes everything here in church, but when he's at school during the week, he has the dirtiest mind. He's the angriest kid in school. He cusses, swears, carries on, acts up, and is abusive. Something's wrong with him."

My mother responded, "What's wrong with *you*? Who do you think you are, coming to me and telling me that? If Paul was actually doing that, he would slip at home. He's never used foul language at home or ever talked like that. He's never been abusive and has never shown any signs of abusive behavior. He's a good boy." My mother argued with people who were telling her the truth because my dual personality was so well developed that I premeditated every word I said in front of my parents and never one time slipped. I had a mask. I could travel with my parents in church work, and they would think I was perfect. I was the compliant "Christian" kid.

We see a duality in ourselves because of the wounds of childhood. The Jekyll-and-Hyde, or dual, personality can begin to show itself as soon as early childhood. It's something we can't control because we can't make decisions and we're locked in the age of directives. We have been so used to living in self-doubt that we have now refined it to a science, and we become a survival personality. In our teen years we see a fulfillment of rejection. Something good could happen to us, but we'll sabotage it and then play the martyr.

Also, we become very selfish—the world seems to revolve around us. As teenagers we start living as a community. We work in a cooperative effort. There are other people here on the earth. They have rights also. When that normal structure of developing community is rebelled against, and we go into an intense self-centeredness and the world revolves around us, you can rest assured we have problems. A normal, healthy teen who is following through in his or her developmental structure will start to be a team player and recognize that there are other people in the world besides himself or herself.

Then the teenager who has been sexually abused feels that promiscuity is the only safe way to connect. *I would rather my body be used than let you know me for who I am. You'll accept my body if I respond to you, but if you really knew me you couldn't accept me. You wouldn't like me.* It's easier to connect through physical relationships than it is to connect through an emotional relationship because the fear of rejection is a greater possibility if you really got to know me. Where there is sexual activity going on, overt sexuality is expressed and then all of a sudden, because of shame, that sexuality diminishes and the teenager isolates, rebels, or both. The teenager hates what he or she has done: promiscuity, isolation, promiscuity. He or she then begins to recycle and start all over again. Teenagers are sensitive, but as the cycle continues to repeat itself, they harden their emotions and then struggle to emotionally bond to others for a lifetime.

Teens may have trouble with anorexia or bulimia. In our denial system as a teen we are able now, by watching other people deny, to deny our situation and blame other people and other situations. At about 18 to 20 years of age we leave home and escape supervision. We can't wait to get out of the house, especially if we have been wounded. We want to be an authority to ourselves. We don't want parents telling us what to do. We don't want a boss telling us how to act. We don't want teachers putting deadlines on us. We don't want a man or woman in our life telling us what to do. That's too much like Mom and Dad.

As wounded adults our barriers are erected, and they're all in place. Our self-doubt is etched in concrete. Our self-esteem is now unattainable unless we get professional help from someone we trust, someone we know who cares for us and who has the ability to access our denial system, give us knowledge and understanding, and stick with us through the rough stuff.

Our rebellion is refined. We now have a hatred of self, and because we hate ourselves, we hate others. To be able to survive we become judgmental. In other words, I have to destroy you and stand on you to be eye-level normal. We then become very critical, very judgmental, and that brings confusion. Because of the fear of love, the fear of knowledge, the doubt of truth, and the wounds that we have experienced as adults, we keep our distance from anything spiritual. We don't want to deal with the church or we become so rigid in our thinking that "rules" will make us perfect. If we follow patterns and man-made rules, we will be accepted by them and maybe by God. Wounded people feel wounded by God. Not all people go to extremes, but many feel they need to prove to God that they're worthy of His attention and love. If we can figure out what love is, we then become performance-oriented; however, there is never enough performance to be loved. We become increasingly independent. We increase promiscuity because it's the only way we know how to connect. We rebel against any and all authority and end up with sexual problems. Then we play these games: "If only," "God knows I've tried," and "Why me?"

As wounded marriage partners, we go into a relationship and start trying to find someone our emotional age to connect with. We call it "love"—but it's sick, trying to get the needs met that we never got met in the family of origin. What happens is that we go into a marriage and end up blocking all of the intimacy that is available. A woman who has experienced problems in childhood will have a tendency to block the intimacy of a husband trying to bond.

I was driving through Nebraska and stopped at a gas station. The words "D.V.P. Learning Center" were on the van I was driving. I walked in to pay the bill for the gas, and one of the two women behind the counter asked, "What does D.V.P. stand for?

I answered, "Domestic Violence Project."

"Where were you last night when I needed you?" she responded.

"What happened?" I asked.

She replied, "Both of our boyfriends started battering us, and now they're in jail."

I asked them, "How many times have you been married?"

Both said they had been married a couple of times.

As wounded marriage partners, we go into a relationship and start trying to find someone our emotional age to connect with.

I said, "Let me ask you a question. Something has happened to you in childhood that made you believe you're not worthy of a good relationship. If you'll play this game with me, I'll ask a question, and you answer me immediately.

"When you were dating before you were first married, a man came along and saw value in you unconditionally. You liked him. He was stable. He was emotionally balanced. He had a good job and had the potential to be a tremendous husband. Because of your feelings about who you are, though, you wanted to date, relate with him, and get to know him, but you blew him off because you felt that if he ever got to know you he would leave you, and you couldn't stand the abandonment feeling."

Instantly both women gave me the names of the men who had made a run at them only to have the women refuse to allow the relationship to develop because of how they felt about themselves.

What happens in a marriage is that we marry in a comfort zone, but we're afraid to get into a relationship with someone who could really care because we feel we're not worthy of that

type of relationship and we'll mess it up. Therefore, we evade
good relationships and settle for second best because of this
issue of our own lack of self-value. Then we end up denying
the problem. We don't want to talk about it. It's simply a total
denial system, and we constantly complain about the situation while we're denying the problem. Life in a marriage relationship will soon come to just such existence, yet we as partners are under an unwritten code that we have to perform, to
prove ourselves. We become performance-oriented. We internalize everything that is going on. A guy will say something,
and she'll internalize. She will say something, and he'll internalize. They are always at each other's throat. We have an addictive type of personality. We isolate even within the marriage. We live with something in our spirit that is a constant
irritability. We have loneliness and distrust. We can be married and have six kids and be as lonely as can be because
we're never connected. We have children, we're married,
we've got bills, we work together—whatever—but we never
connect. Then we live with thoughts of suicide and hopelessness. We deal with fear and anxiety. We express ourselves
many times in a safe way (we think) in hostile humor, nag-
ging, criticism, defensiveness, and we're angry all the time.
Anger does not come out of a vacuum; it has a source. You
may have crying spells and provoking. For instance, if I could
provoke Judy and she would react by screaming and yelling
and crying, I knew I had her hooked. When I would try to
provoke and she ignored me, the message I got was that she
had fallen out of love. I don't have her under control any
more. Provocation is a test to see if you're still hooked, and if
you're still hooked, I'm safe. You won't leave me.

    Then we end up with a life of trying to control others and
trying to control situations. We become good at manipulating
and using any power and control method that works. We end
up just trying to survive. Since we have no control over ourselves, the way we survive is by trying to control all the situations around us. We try to control the people around us because if we can control others, it helps build our self-esteem

(we think). If I can control my boss, someone in the church, my wife and my family, then my world is safe. If I can control circumstances, situations, and people, that makes me feel safe, because I have no self-control. We allow no emotions to come to the surface. We live with things of a compulsive type of nature. It will come out in various addictions as we have no ability to cope. We are possibly very tired because we never rest. We're always "on." The adrenaline is always rolling. We live in a shame base that says "I'm bad," and we take that as gospel truth, which says we have no ability to change. Our decisions are made by indecision, circumstances, and other people. With this set-up for life, we'll end up divorcing and marrying again and again, repeating the same patterns. We'll always get less than we deserve; yet our mind wants change. The only way we can live is with the hope of a better tomorrow. However, most of the time our attitudes and our verbalization to others and ourselves is hopelessness. We live with the feeling that we're never worthy of anything good. I am totally insecure and will end up being alone. I am frustrated in every area of my life.

SET UP FOR LIFE

These destructive patterns set us up for life. In our dysfunction we don't leave one stage and graduate to the next. Sadly, we drag all our baggage with us, collecting more along the way. We go through life getting less than we deserve because we desperately want change but have no hope for it. With the passage of time we feel more unworthy, insecure, and frustrated. We have little ability to cope, and we live in a mode of exhaustion and depression. We're filled with shame as we model this behavior to our children. This cycle repeats itself in our children and grandchildren. Eventually it becomes our norm for living.

We can use the above description as a diagnostic of where we're stuck and how life has responded due to the arrest in our development. The sooner we understand these things, the sooner we can start the maturing process and be the person God intended us to be. We can take control of our lives and understand where we got stuck. We can allow the trust to start to develop. This is the beginning of character development and the journey to normalcy.

Chapter 7

SHAME, GUILT, AND ANGER

SHAME AND GUILT—WHAT'S THE DIFFERENCE?

Can we ever leave our reactive baggage behind? Yes. It will require work, but time is our friend. The first step in the process is to understand the difference between shame and guilt.

If I don't know the difference between shame and guilt, I will never be able to find and understand my value as a person. Shame is the perception that locks me into a belief system that says, "I'm bad. I'm wrong. I'm no good." It comes out of a tendency toward perfectionism and leads to the expectation of rejection, rigidity, isolation, and despair. When I operate from a shame-based worldview, my value is buried under my dysfunctions, fears, anxieties, behaviors, mistakes, imperfections, rejections, feelings, powerlessness, and sins. I am satisfied with nothing less than perfection. I live on a performance basis and place unrealistic expectations on my partner and those around me as well as myself. No matter what I do, I feel I'm never good enough.

Shame and rage are interactive—where there is rage there is shame. Rage comes from helplessness. It hides shame. Rage keeps a person from being exposed. It is isolating and disconnecting.

Anger, which is not the same as rage, is a way of expressing feelings in order to connect and repair the relationship with another person.

Shame is a learned behavior. We weren't born with it. Rather, we learn it from various sources, such as our family of origin, school, relationships, culture, and even church.

Guilt, on the other hand, can be a healthful emotion that a person with a strong value system experiences. It is based on a presumption that says, *I made a mistake. I did a bad thing. My attitude or behavior was wrong, or I have sinned. But I am a person of worth and infinite value.* When my core value is in place, I have the ability to change my attitudes, behaviors, reactions, and actions. In other words, I'm in control of myself. When I function in a guilt-based system (as opposed to a shame-based system), I grow in accountability and responsibility. My self-worth deepens, and my character is formed. I can build a healthy belief system on a firm foundation. My mistakes and failures become learning experiences. They do not reflect my self-worth. I have the power of choice to change attitudes and behaviors.

Guilt can be atoned for because the promise of love is still there and we can experience the relief of being forgiven. It has a beginning and a possible ending. Guilt is about your *behavior*. Shame is about *you*. Guilt can be a learning tool, but shame blocks learning. Shame and blame go together and can be aimed at self or at others.

The shame produced by the wounds of childhood can be processed to guilt, just as the caterpillar becomes a butterfly. Discovering the sources of our shame is the beginning of that transformation.

GUILT IS ABOUT YOUR BEHAVIOR. SHAME IS ABOUT YOU.

The shame-based person fears punishment, abandonment, and rejection. He or she feels overly responsible for circumstances. Shame is the byproduct of the way a person is treated. *I was treated as though I were worthless; therefore I must be worthless* might be the thought. Part of the healing process is to recognize the shame as a truth of the past but not as a truth about the person today. We live in a shame-based society. The shame produced by the wounds of childhood can be processed to guilt, just as the caterpillar becomes a butterfly. Discovering the sources of our shame is the beginning of that transformation. Consider the following steps that can start you on your journey to freedom:

- Identify the wounds of childhood—almost everyone has something in childhood that hurts. It can range from minor things on the surface to major deep pain or wounds. We can't always remember them clearly. If the memory has faded, don't go digging into the past. The memories will surface when you're ready and able to process them.
- Identify the reactive behaviors that undermine our values and perpetuate the shame. We can tell by our reactive behaviors if there's been a wound in childhood. We may have lost the memory consciously, but the wound will unconsciously drive our behavior. I started recovery without the memories coming to the surface by identifying the behaviors and changing them. It is a process.
- Recognize that with the shame there comes pain. This is normal. Journal or log the feelings you've associated with each incident. Stay with the process. The pain will eventually diminish, and you'll see light at the end of the tunnel.
- If the pain or the fear associated with the incidents is too much to handle, get help. A trusted friend, family member, or your pastor may or may not be the place to start. There should be no shame in seeking professional help.
- Focus on growth, which develops maturity of character. If we are arrested in our development, we have never developed our core and character. Our personality is a pseudopersonality, and much behavior modification will not work long-term. As we focus on the development of character, we grow from the inside, and behavior changes over time. Then the change can be permanent.
- Become future-oriented instead of dwelling on the

past. Choose to live in the solution instead of perpet-
uating the problem. Look forward. As we mature we
can take control of our lives and let go of situations,
circumstances, and other people. We can achieve our
dreams, goals, and visions.

- Determine to do everything you can to stop the behaviors connected to the wound. When we identify a
  negative behavior, look for the opposite behavior and
  focus on change. Do not try to change everything at
  once. Time is our friend. It took many of us years to
  get this way, and the recovery process might take the
  rest of our lives. But it does get progressively better.

Continue to grow over the long term by using positive,
self-valuing statements, finding a support system, and focus-
ing on spiritual growth.

For the batterer, containment (taking responsibility and
initiative to stop the behavior) is primary. This is true for the
emotional abuser as well as the physical abuser. For the victim, safety is primary (removing herself from the situation using the resources of the community such as marital separation
and counsel, shelter, order of protection, law enforcement).

If you are a woman caught in emotional abuse, there's another way out: as you discover your value, you're empowered
to make decisions and take healthy control of your life. You're
free to discover the person God has created you to be. The
healing process has begun.

THE ANGER KIT

After we've discovered the source of our shame, we can expect two responses: pain and anger. Our individual anger pattern as an adult is usually a refinement of the anger patterns
we learned in childhood. If Dad screamed and threw things
when he was displeased, that will be my mode. His model
gives me permission to act out in his way. It seems to work. My
wife and children skitter around to obey my every command
and fix my problems when I raise my voice. I am in control.

Even if I determine to reject my father's model, I have to unlearn and reshape my anger response. Otherwise, it will manifest itself in other areas, such as control, manipulation, rigidity, or avoiding the conflict altogether. When I get mad, I may not throw things and yell—I give my family the cold shoulder and the silent treatment instead. My wife and children work harder to please me and fix my problems. I am in control. And despite my determination not to be like him, I have embraced my father's anger model without even knowing it.

For insight into our emotional reactions, it is best to look at least two generations back into the family of origin. Understanding how your parents and grandparents acted out their anger can give you a clue to your own responses.

Understanding Anger Patterns in Your Family of Origin

1. How did your parents act out their anger?

2. How did your parents react to each other's anger?

3. How did your grandparents act out their anger?

4. How did your grandparents react to each other's anger?

5. How did your parents handle conflict—was it resolved or avoided?

6. Were you afraid during your parents' expressions of anger?

7. Were you allowed to express anger as a child?

8. How did you express anger as a child?

9. How do you express anger now?

10. If you could, how would you change your responses to your anger?

Our individual anger patterns as adults are usually merely fluffed-up versions of our childhood anger patterns (learned behavior). They are fairly "set" or "fixed." As a result, they are also predictable. People who know us well know just the right "buttons" to push to get the anger responses they wish to provoke.

However, because these patterns were learned, they can be unlearned and reshaped. We can decide what we want our pattern to be by adjusting our expectations and responses. Anger is a universal, basic, normal, unavoidable reaction of displeasure. It usually involves a significant portion of misunderstanding and has its roots in our own unmet expectations. It generates an internally created, increased physical force that we control or fail to control as we choose.

Anger is a secondary emotion; more basic emotions underlie it. It entails contradiction of a belief or self-concept. Our anger responses are patterned and programmed; we were taught by example how to respond. Because responses are internally created, they can be internally managed. They are most often expressed toward those who are meaningful to us.

Anger is an emotional reaction to certain kinds of stress-producing situations. Anger is not a primary emotion, but is rather a secondary reactive response. More basic emotions underlie it, such as in the Anger Model (see Figure 7).

When we become angry, we react impulsively. Without delayed responses or impulse control, we will trigger and go directly to our learned reactive behavior, which is generally aggression. Anger and aggression are different in that while aggression is intended to cause injury or harm, anger gives us strength, determination, and sometimes satisfaction. It has desirable as well as undesirable effects. Our purpose is to decrease the negative effects and increase the positive ones.

Anger occurs at different levels of intensity. A small amount can be used constructively; however, high degrees of anger seldom produce positive results. Getting very mad or losing our temper prevents us from thinking clearly. We may then say or do things that we will later regret.

Anger is a universal, basic, normal, unavoidable reaction of displeasure. It usually involves a significant portion of misunderstanding and has its roots in our own unmet expectations.

Aggression can get you into trouble. When we feel we've been taken advantage of in one way or another, we want to lash out at the person who offended us, even though that person may be the one who is closest and dearest to us. Sometimes we choose to explode before we think of the consequences to ourselves or to others.

Anger does not automatically become aggression. Wanting to hit someone and actually doing it are two different responses. Sometimes we hit the other person because it is the only way we know how to act. This is abuse and is the wrong way of dealing with our anger. Our anger responses are patterned and programmed—we were taught how to respond in childhood.

One of the most important things to do is to control your anger by recognizing your signs of tension, both internal and external. As you learn your trigger points and trigger signs, you can learn to relax, and your ability to handle anger will improve. Because anger is internally created, it can be internally managed.

Understanding the underlying causes for anger is the first step in resolution. When we recognize the anger and the initial hurt, we then have options to handle the feelings and resolve the conflict. Let's look at the options:

Attack

Although it may dissipate the energy, an attack does not resolve the conflict. It will burn off the adrenaline, but it leaves the issue open-ended. This approach may also have consequences (such as broken relationships, arrest, detachment, rejection, and so on).

Denial/Running

To deny the situation and run from it leaves us with a feeling of helplessness and weakness. We feel victimized once more. We have no control over our lives. We are at the mercy of everyone else. This creates fear and anxiety.

Holding a Grudge

It stresses the body to hold a grudge. The blood pressure rises, the heart rate increases, and muscles become and remain tense. It places strain on the mind and body. We are more susceptible to further aggravation. It becomes easier to get angry the next time something triggers us.

Giving In

If we feel we are always the victim, this prolongs our anger. We collect the injustices, play the martyr, and live in the past. Anger is prolonged when we remind ourselves of past incidents that have upset us. When they are unresolved, we be-

FIGURE 7
ANGER MODEL

EXPECTATION   TRIGGER

"Life Commandments"	Ego Bruise	Primary Feeling	Secondary Feeling
Others should always be kind, considerate, and fair to me; they should understand me.	You don't like me.	Hurt Resentment	Anger
Others should always be prompt, honest, and reasonable toward me. They should respect me.	You aren't being fair to me.	Disappointment Discouragement	Anger
I should always understand, take charge, be decisive, and initiate action.	I don't comprehend this.	Confusion Frustration	Anger
I should always be competent, efficient, right, assertive, compassionate, articulate, perfect. (Shame-based)	I'm not doing a good job.	Inadequacy Insecurity	Anger
I should always be motivated, enthusiastic, positive.	My attitude is bad.	Dejection (Hopelessness)	Anger
I should always be in control, be self-directed, have faith, believe in myself, achieve.	Conditions are too much for me.	Helplessness	Anger
I should always be courageous, confident, brave, strong, a model.	I can't handle this.	Fear Anxiety	Anger
I should never make mistakes, backslide, put myself first, hurt others.	If I'm not perfect, I'm not a good person.	Shame	Anger
Others should respect me, my decisions, opinions, and my choices. If they don't, then they don't like me.	I'm not an acceptable person.	Rejection Loneliness	Anger
I should use the skills that I have learned in life.	I made a big mistake.	Guilt Sadness	Anger

SITUATION

Adapted from James Moore, *Modern Learning Systems* (Minneapolis: self-published, 1981).

gin the anger process all over again in our minds. Memories of things that were unresolved can bring back our anger vividly, and it becomes a reality again and again.

RESOLUTION

Step 1: Take a Time-Out

Impulse control is not a natural attribute; it is a learned behavior. It starts with delaying our responses. The moment you feel the escalation of emotions leading to anger, you need to take a time-out and define what you're really feeling (hurt, rejection, helplessness, shame, guilt, or whatever else it might be). Consider using the Time-Out Contract (Figure 8).

Step 2: Recognize Your Feelings

Evaluate how upset you are and where this escalation could lead. How destructive could this be if you allow it to get out of control?

Step 3: Identify the True Cause of the Anger

What triggered it? What were the circumstances that created the emotions you're dealing with right now? What is the reality of the situation?

Step 4: Evaluate the Anger

Is the anger legitimate, or did you perceive the situation wrong? Many times because of your wounds of childhood, your sensitivity, fears, anxieties, and rejection factors, you perceive things and experience feelings that are not necessarily reality. Step back from the situation and even get a reality check from a friend before taking action.

Step 5: Think Through the Situation

Do not take action until you have thought through the situation and have control of your responses, reactions, and words.

Step 6: Resolve the Conflict

After thinking clearly and seeing the reality of the con-

FIGURE 8

TIME-OUT CONTRACT

1. The cues that indicate I am getting angry are

   _____   _____

   _____   _____

   _____   _____

2. The "triggers" (red flags) that I need to avoid are

   _____   _____

   _____   _____

3. The neutral, nonblaming time-out signal that I will use will be

   _____

4. When I give the above signal, I will go _____

   _____

5. When my partner gives the time-out signal, I will abide by the contract.

6. The time-out period will last for _____ [at least 60] minutes.

7. At the end of the time-out period, we will _____

   _____

8. During the time-out period, I will observe the following rules:
   [no caffeine, drugs, or alcohol]_____

   _____

   _____

   SIGNED _____

   WITNESS _____ DATE _____

flict, you have many choices by which to resolve the conflict. You can confront calmly, set boundaries and limits, get unbiased wise counsel, express the feelings, negotiate resolution, compromise—or pass over the issue until a later time. You can simply let go. You have no control over other people, situations, or circumstances.

Step 7: Forgive

Forgiveness releases you from the mental grip of the person who offended you. Forgiveness does not condone the behavior of the perpetrator. Many times the perpetrator's response is a false or pseudorepentance, so it does not require the other person to acknowledge what he or she has done. Forgiveness itself breaks the bond. Forgiveness does not require you to reestablish relationship with the offender. Forgiveness does not mean you have to go back and receive a second offense. You can forgive and yet set boundaries. Forgiveness starts the process of diminishing pain. The choice of forgiveness starts a process that takes time for the sting to be released from the memory of the event. You will probably never forget, but the pain will diminish.

The Process of Forgiveness

- Identify the event or trauma.
- Identify the person connected to that event.
- Choose to forgive.
- Identify your reactive behaviors connected to the event.
- Share the pain with someone you really trust.
- Focus on growth that develops character and maturity.
- Choose to stop the behaviors connected to the event.
- Maintain growth by positive self-talk, reaffirmation, and value statements.

This process creates a finish line in the mind. Closure begins the healing process.

Chapter 8

BUILDING HEALTHY RELATIONSHIPS

Building healthy relationships is possible. The keys are knowledge, commitment, and the willingness to exercise building trust.

To begin, we need to understand what a normal, healthy relationship really is. If we've been raised in a home with dysfunction or if our development has been arrested by trauma, we probably don't have any models to emulate.

We've already seen that relationships built around power and control eventually self-destruct. Healthy relationships are built around respect and freedom and thrive over the years. Examining some of the components of healthy relationships will enable us to (1) develop our identity, (2) begin the emotional bonding process, and (3) build relationships with people we choose, not people we need.

We looked at the Varieties of Abuse Wheel in chapter 2. The Healthy Relationship Wheel (Figure 9) is the opposite of that. The components of a healthy relationship are as follows.

Appropriate Touching

Appropriate touching finds value in nonsexual hugs and the expression of the need to be touched. It is the ability to express the frequency of the touching and the extent of the touching. This is very important. For instance, it is not easy for a woman who has just come home from a day's work and is preparing supper for her family to respond when her husband walks up and starts touching her sexually. She has other things on her mind.

FIGURE 9

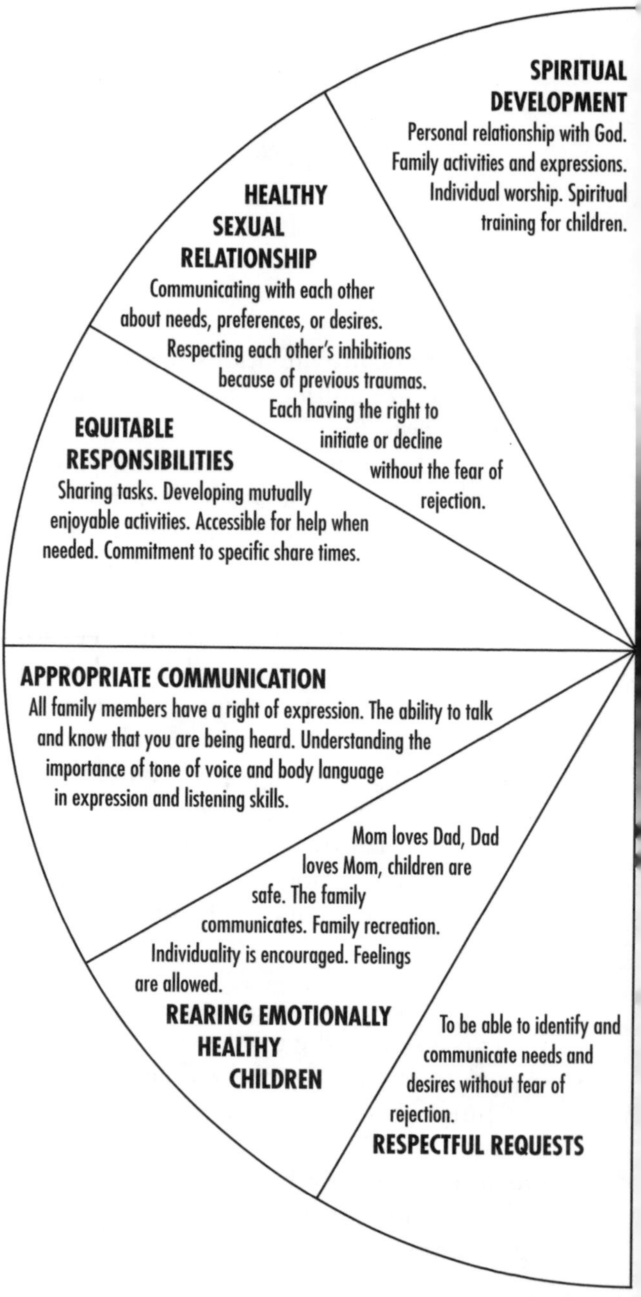

SPIRITUAL DEVELOPMENT
Personal relationship with God. Family activities and expressions. Individual worship. Spiritual training for children.

HEALTHY SEXUAL RELATIONSHIP
Communicating with each other about needs, preferences, or desires. Respecting each other's inhibitions because of previous traumas. Each having the right to initiate or decline without the fear of rejection.

EQUITABLE RESPONSIBILITIES
Sharing tasks. Developing mutually enjoyable activities. Accessible for help when needed. Commitment to specific share times.

APPROPRIATE COMMUNICATION
All family members have a right of expression. The ability to talk and know that you are being heard. Understanding the importance of tone of voice and body language in expression and listening skills.

Mom loves Dad, Dad loves Mom, children are safe. The family communicates. Family recreation. Individuality is encouraged. Feelings are allowed.

REARING EMOTIONALLY HEALTHY CHILDREN

To be able to identify and communicate needs and desires without fear of rejection.

RESPECTFUL REQUESTS

APPROPRIATE TOUCHING
Valuing through nonsexual hugs. Ability to express the need to be touched—frequency and extent.

PROPER BONDING
Emotional support. A composite of two perceptions allowing for individuality, yet creating a new entity called "we." Building esteem and value.

ECONOMIC COOPERATION
Mutual consent for major spending. Open communication on financial matters great or small.

RESPECT OF PROPERTY
A respect for the relationship, her property, his property, and mutual property, with regard to individual property of each of the children.

Acceptable public displays of affection. Checking first before making commitments for both. Being structured and scheduled versus being spontaneous.
APPROPRIATE SOCIAL BEHAVIORS

The right to personal space. Personal interests, activities, decisions, friends, and growth activities. The right to decline dislikes.
APPROPRIATE INDIVIDUALITY

Kevin Leman, a Christian psychologist in Tucson, Arizona, makes the statement on the video *Battle of the Sexes*[1] that many times a woman does not approach and voluntarily hug her husband because within 1.7 seconds of her move toward him, he is interpreting it sexually. Women sometimes need nonsexual validating and nonsexual hugging. If she trusts and knows that she can be valued nonsexually and it's safe to get a hug, she then starts to respond to him in a more sexual way. It's all about a trust factor. The touching and the hugging and the nonsexual approach are very important in a relationship.

Proper Bonding

Proper bonding starts with emotional support. As an example, let's look at the difference between a male and a female in emotional support.

She comes home from work, sits down for supper, and says, "I tell you—I've had the worst day I've ever had in my whole life. I went in this morning, met every deadline, and had a report on the boss's desk like he wanted, yet he yelled at me because it wasn't fast enough. I've never had a day like I've had today!"

He either says, "Well, you ought to have seen my day if you think your day was bad!" or "Aw—that's no big deal. I don't know why you're so upset about it. You know, the boss probably was having a bad day. Maybe his wife upset him before he left for work, or he had an accident on the way, or he ran out of gas. Something must have happened."

In this situation, what the wife needs is emotional support. Yet her husband seems to support the enemy, the one who is abusing her emotionally on the job or has yelled at her. Her partner not only makes excuses for the person who has wounded her but also makes her feel guilty for being so emotional. When he sticks up for the boss who has done the damage and wounded her spirit, she wonders, "Am I nuts? Is my perception out of whack?" It creates self-doubt. She should be able to come home and share freely what she has gone through. Instead of getting into a contest about who had the worst day, he could say, "You're handling those problems quite well. I could understand how you'd feel if I had a day that bad." He supports her, and she doesn't think she's crazy.

Emotional support is a very integral part of the bonding in the relationship. Bonding is emotionally supporting, caring, listening, and sharing the depths of feelings.

Two Perceptions

We have to understand that a married couple is a composite of two perceptions. The brain stores a seemingly unlimited number of memories. Out of these memories come our pain, our joy, our perceptions, our opinions, and our biases. A marriage relationship is the combination of two perceptions, allowing for individuality and opinions, yet creating the broadness of a new entity as the couple comes together and is called "we." In other words, instead of his molding her to meet his needs and wanting her to think like him—or her doing the same to him—they recognize their perceptions, which are totally different. This gives them broader exposure to what is going on in their life as a couple. I want Judy to keep her opinions and develop identity, character, and autonomy, and I should encourage her to be what she needs to be. She has a perspective, and I have a perspective, so when we see an issue or an attack, we can see all angles of it. She sees sides of it that I do not. I see sides of it that she does not. That's what can build a relationship. I am still an individual, and I am growing in my own way. She is also growing in her way. However, together we have created a very broad entity called "we," who can go out and face the world if we do it together.

Economic Cooperation

A couple should have mutual consent for major spending and open communications on financial matters great or small. In other words, both partners should know where they stand financially at any given time, and that creates stability and a safety factor as they work together in that area. Areas of discussion can be as follows: proportional sharing of expenses, the need for personal "nonaccountable" funds, veto power on debt commitments, and mutual consent for major purchases.

Respect of Property

This includes respect of the relationship, her property, his property, mutual property, and the property of each child. In other words, men do not own everything. There are things that she may have that are really her things—like china, personal items, the stereo she got for Christmas, or the car that's in her name. That's fine. A man also might have things that are really his—like tools, lawn equipment, or the stereo he got for Christmas. But still some things are theirs, and she should be allowed to go out to the toolbox and pick up what she needs to hang a picture and know that she's not going to get battered. (Likewise, he should be allowed to play a compact disc on her stereo without complaint.) We respect each other's property.

When our children were at home, they thought they had their own property, but as their dad I had the mind-set that "what is theirs is mine too." I told them how to use it, what to do with it, when to play with it, and when to throw it away. However, in a balanced home the respect of property allows the children and the couple to grow individually and acquire things that they can be stewards of. This especially applies to children in learning how to take care of their things. That is also a part of what a happy home is about.

Appropriate Social Behaviors

Appropriate social behaviors include acceptable public displays of affection. If a partner was sexually abused in childhood, she may be sensitive to many types of public displays of affection. Any type of touching in public can then be perceived as inappropriate and cause withdrawal. These are areas in a relationship that the couple needs to discuss.

Appropriate Individuality

Identity, autonomy, and intimacy all go together in a balanced relationship. We should be a couple by choice, not because we need to force the partner to meet our needs. Each person in the relationship needs personal space and freedom to develop personal interests. We need activities and friendships together as a family, yet each may want or need individual activities, friends, or growth activities. As an individual, a person should be able to decline something he or she doesn't want to do and not have to fear rejection. This is an important part of a healthy relationship.

Respectful Requests

To be able to identify and communicate needs and desires without fear of rejection is what it means to have respectful requests. Again, we need to be mature enough to be able to identify those needs and express them.

Many couples set themselves up for disaster by expecting the other person to be able to read his or her mind and meet the projected needs. If I do not even know what I need or cannot identify it, my partner might be trying to meet the need he or she perceives. But the need still doesn't get identified, so I can't recognize the effort, and the partner never has a finish line. My needs are getting met, but I didn't know my need and the effort of the partner was wasted. I'm still needy.

When the needs are actually identified, we should talk about them and not feel rejected if the communication or the response doesn't go the way we think it should at that moment. Remember—we are dealing with perspectives, and a healthy relationship allows for individuality and perspectives.

Rearing Emotionally Healthy Children

Mom loves Dad, and Dad loves Mom, and the children are safe. The family communicates. But as is the case in so many situations today, many families are separated through marital separation or divorce. The father might say to the child, "Honey, I love you, and I always will. I'll always be your father." The mother may say basically the same thing to the child. Yet the child doesn't respond. Those statements are not as comforting to a child as the security of the love of the father for the mother and the mother for the father. When the child realizes that Mom and Dad love each other and are committed to each other by resolving conflicts, communicating, nurturing, and bonding, the child then feels safe and secure, knowing the home is a safe place in which to live.

For instance, the family has recreation time together. It is during the recreation time that the child sees the bonding and the way the family interrelates. The child sees team effort, competition, negotiations, closeness, communication, sharing, touching, goal setting, excitement, rewards, and closeness. This creates security. Individuality is encouraged and feelings are allowed, and even the feelings of children are treated with respect. If we do not respect the feelings of children, they will grow up to feel that *I have no value, and nobody wants to hear me.* The child will grow to an adult who will repress feelings and act out in many ways just to get attention, hoping that someone will see the pain and come to the rescue. We must develop the ability to deal with the feelings of a child and bring that child into maturity in a safe home.

Appropriate Communication

All family members should have a right of expression and the ability to talk and to know that they are being heard and understood. Understanding the importance of tone of voice and body language in expression is a listening skill. Children differ in the ways they hear, speak, and communicate. Some are more audio-oriented or verbally oriented. Some are very "huggie-touchie" and need physical attention, while others are very visual-oriented. Parents need to identify the dominance of each child and try to communicate with that child in his or her style.

Equitable Responsibilities

The idea of equitable responsibilities includes sharing tasks, developing mutually enjoyable activities, negotiating, being accessible for help when needed, committing to specific share times, supporting each other's goals, undertaking couple growth programs together, and even pledging to attend counseling if needed. The healthy family shares the power within the family. No one has all the power.

Healthy Sexual Relationships

Healthy sexual relationships are extremely important. They include the ability to communicate with each other about needs, preferences, or desires, plus respecting each other's inhibitions because of previous traumas, each having the right to initiate or decline without the fear of rejection.

If a woman has been damaged sexually in childhood and her husband demands the type of sexual activity that was forced upon her, he will put himself in the role of her childhood perpetrator and she will have a tendency to withdraw sexually from him. Until she has an understanding of these issues and dynamics and is comfortable with that type of lovemaking, she needs to be able to express that she is not comfortable in that area—and not be rejected for doing so. If her husband forces the issue, she will see him in a different light until that issue has been settled. Many times she shuts off totally in her sexual responses because she sees him as the perpetrator.

Spiritual Development

Spiritual development includes our personal and family relationship with God. It includes family activities within the home and at the place of worship, our personal expressions of worship, respect of individual worship and denomination, the definition of our participation, our financial commitment to the faith and church, the definition of our belief systems and traditions, and the spiritual training of the children. The spiritual tide of the home should be mutual. Both partners should have input in this area.

STEPS TO A HEALTHY RELATIONSHIP

Recognize the Power of Attraction to the Opposite Sex

Attraction to the opposite sex is what brings a couple together. Men are attracted physically to a woman. A woman responds, if she's emotionally healthy, not to the looks of a man so much as to the depth of his character.

Some ministers have said, "You know, I don't know what to do with this dynamic. Every once in a while a woman will walk through my life, and I'll have this desperate attraction to her. What's wrong with me? I'm a man of God. I'm a minister. Why am I attracted to her? Why does this bother me so much? Why am I sinning?"

Attraction to the opposite sex is not a sin; it's a natural, physical, emotional reaction. However, the marriage covenant includes a commitment to close the heart, mind, and eyes to things that may violate that promise. After marriage, attraction to members of the opposite sex is temptation. It is what we do with this temptation that makes it a sin. I have the 72-hour rule. If somebody comes through your life and there is an attraction, do not think about it for three days. When it comes back to your mind, you will see reality, and the attraction will usually be gone.

The same rule holds true in dealing with pain. If you are feeling emotionally pained about something in life and the wound hurts desperately, walk through that pain and realize where it is coming from and deal with it. Within 72 hours that pain should start to diminish, and you should see the light at the end of the tunnel.

It is based on this: Friday was an extremely painful day for Jesus, but Sunday came. He entered His pain, but by Sunday there was victory. I challenge you to test the 72-hour rule. If you enter your pain and stick with it for 72 hours, you should start to see relief.

In the midst of the 72 hours, know where your commitments are. Try to have this attitude: "I know where I'm going. I know that I've committed everything to God. My whole life is His."

Develop a Friendship

There are four levels of friendship: (1) acquaintance; (2)

casual; (3) close; (4) intimate. A frequent problem is that too many acquaintances are entrusted to an intimate level of friendship. For instance, you venture to share a secret. Three days later you hear the secret back from other people. Then you feel betrayed. You shared too much of yourself with someone with whom you had not taken time to develop a close friendship. Consider who your friends are, and place them at the proper level of friendship for the type of relationship you have with them.

A frequent problem is that too many acquaintances are entrusted to an intimate level of friendship.

Judy and I were not friends in our first marriage. We were acquaintances who were married and living and sleeping together. Yet we had nothing in common. In our second courtship we started out at the acquaintance level then went to casual. When we got closer, she started to trust me. Then we were able to talk about the past and eventually a possible future. In this process I discovered things about Judy I had never known—not in the entire time we were together in our first marriage to each other.

These are the skills for building or restoring a relationship. Become friends. Become safe in the ability to express yourself, your needs, and your pain, and know that you are safe to do that. Neither of you should be in a reactive mode. After the issues are identified, you can work through that intimate level of friendship. Here's a little more insight into our experience of reacquainting ourselves with each other.

As our relationship was developing, I sat down with a couple of legal pads one night. I was feeling things about Judy that I had never felt, even when we dated the first time. So I did a personal inventory. If we were to get together again, what did I need to bring to the table? What negatives was I dealing with? What were my issues? What am I going to struggle with as we pair? This was long before we discussed remarriage, but I started getting quite transparent with myself, because I was about ready to involve somebody else in my life.

During this period, Judy and I often met at Denny's Restaurant. She wouldn't meet me anywhere else, but Denny's was a safe place. She wouldn't let me pick her up. She drove, so if she got scared by my behavior, she could get into her car and drive home. I had no power, no control of her ability to escape. I sat on the side of the booth farthest from the door so she could feel that she could leave freely.

The continued bonding in a relationship is an ongoing process.

Later we started going out in a group. I wouldn't go pick her up yet, because she was still afraid. But eventually we moved to the point at which I would pick her up. We were pairing, but we were in a crowd, so she was safe. Then we started the exclusive one-on-one dating game. We talked about marriage or remarriage; we defined love. We discussed what love is and what it is not, mature love and immature love. We could see what we were dealing with as we started to get into a relationship and move into something that had potential.

The continued bonding in a relationship is an ongoing process. The individuals invest themselves in the value of each other in an established nonsexual way. That's the biblical standard. She feels secure because she knows she is loved for who she is, and it is two individuals again, coming together and forming the new entity called "we."

At the marriage altar the commitment has been made, her value has been established, and if the relationship is properly built, sexuality and bonding will last a lifetime. The thing we men need to understand is that this emotional bonding should not stop. As long as we continue to invest ourselves in our partner's life, as men, it will pay off not only in your relationship with your wife but also in how your children respond.

The best thing you can do for your children is to love your spouse. The best things you can do as a couple for your kids include building a relationship, resolving conflict, managing anger, and becoming stable, responsible, and accountable. Kids are resilient, and when they see Mom and Dad working it out, they're thrilled. So be honest and take a new path.

FIGURE 10

STEPS TO A HEALTHY RELATIONSHIP

SEXUAL INTIMACY
If relationship is properly built, sexuality and bonding will last a lifetime.

COMMITMENT/MARRIAGE
Her value has been established; she feels secure and knows she is loved for *who* she is. Two individuals coming together forming a new entity called "we."

EMOTIONAL BONDING
[engagement]
Usually no longer than one year.
An ongoing process.

LOVE DEFINED
[Going Steady]
What is love?
Do I want to invest myself in this person?

RELATIONSHIP
8. Exclusive   (One-on-one)
7. Multiple   (Group — pairing)
6. Multiple   (Group — no pairing)
5. Me to Me   (Time out to evaluate what I bring to the relationship)

FRIENDSHIP
4. Intimate
3. Close
2. Casual
1. Acquaintance

GIFT OF ATTRACTION

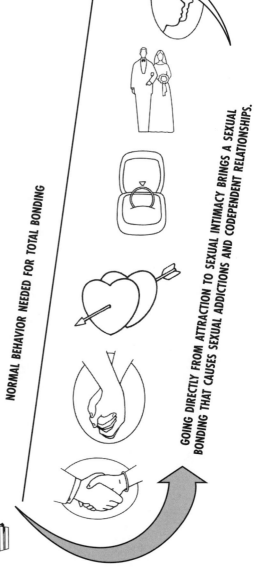

NORMAL BEHAVIOR NEEDED FOR TOTAL BONDING

GOING DIRECTLY FROM ATTRACTION TO SEXUAL INTIMACY BRINGS A SEXUAL BONDING THAT CAUSES SEXUAL ADDICTIONS AND CODEPENDENT RELATIONSHIPS.

Adapted from Bill Gothard, Institute in Basic Life Principles, Oak Brook, Ill. Also Jim Talley, *Friends* (self-published, 1992). Also Desmond Morris, *Intimate Behavior: A Zoologist's Classic Study of Human Intimacy* (New York: Random House, 1971).

FOR REFLECTION

How does your relationship measure up? Do you recognize yourself in the cycle of unhealthy relationship? If so, you may feel trapped. Take heart. You have nothing to lose and everything to gain by being transparent. Consider the answers to some of the most commonly asked questions by people who may be just like you.

Consider the following stigmas of the abused woman:

Being Alone

Many of us feel that being alone is evidence of not being wanted, loved, or accepted. In reality these feelings stem from our own fear of rejection, lack of value or self-esteem, and the way we have been treated all our life.

Each of us was created with value and significance. Read these words from Ps. 139:

You did form my inward parts; You did knit me together in my mother's womb. I will confess and praise You for You are fearful and wonderful and for the awful wonder of my birth! Wonderful are Your works, and that my inner self knows right well. My frame was not hidden from You when I was being formed in secret [and] intricately and curiously wrought [as if embroidered with various colors] in the depths of the earth [a region of darkness and mystery]. Your eyes saw my unformed substance, and in Your book all the days [of my life] were written before ever they took shape, when as yet there was none of them (*vv. 13-16*, AMP.).

Judy. Speaking as someone who has been married and basically became a clone of my spouse, I was attached or had my value in being with my husband. When it all came tumbling down, it was as if I had been a Siamese twin severed with no identity of my own. It was frightening to be alone, because I had been a puppet with no real mind of my own, and I wasn't sure I could make it on my own. Yet I did, and I found strengths I didn't know I had.

Being Single/Divorced

Being single and/or divorced has always carried with it a stigma in the church and in society. Implications are that "I'm less of a person without a mate"; "I must be a bad person because I couldn't keep my partner happy"; "I probably didn't try hard enough to make things work." Remember that these statements may not necessarily be what others are saying but may be something we're feeling because of what we've been taught. In your own mind you have to come to the realization that you did everything humanly possible to make things work. Let go of these thoughts, and stop blaming yourself.

Being Abused

As stated earlier, victimization usually starts in early childhood. Many times abuse comes from within the family of origin; for some women and girls the abuse comes from outside the family. Often abuse can come from both places, putting victims into a double bind. The shame-based family is not a safe place in which the victim can resolve the wounds. Shame-based families do not talk, do not feel, and do not trust, so children do not and cannot receive the validation, nurturing, and understanding that lead to the healing process. The children are cheated out of the knowledge that the trauma or abuse was the responsibility and the sin of the perpetrators, not of their own. Without such freeing knowledge, the children have been set up to be victims for the rest of their lives, always living in self-doubt and assuming lifetime responsibility for the continuing abuse. To overcome this stigma, we need to recognize that there is a source for our feelings, but the reality is that we are still intact with the ability to take control of our lives and direct new paths, by choice. This process requires knowledge, understanding, and a support system.

Being Penniless

As stated in earlier chapters, arrested development manifests itself at a crisis point. The shame of being broke or poor and being at the mercy of a controlling spouse can be paralyzing, and we live in tremendous fear and anxiety. With this dynamic present in our lives, we feel we have lost control of ourselves, there is no way out, we have no options, we are at the mercy of someone else, we're embarrassed, we feel like a child. With all of this we're scared, because we used to have financial support, and now we're on our own. Questions keep coming up such as "How am I going to make it?" "Will I be able to get and keep a job?" "Will I be able to support myself and the children?" We feel not only paralyzed but almost hopeless.

This is the time that you have permission to take control of your life, to be creative and realize that you're an individual with value. Develop friendships that can give you encouragement and possibly help you develop options. Remember: developing the right friendships can be your first step in overcoming the stigmas.

QUESTIONS FROM ABUSED WOMEN

Will God still love me if I leave my spouse?

Yes! Divorce is not the unpardonable sin. He will always love us for *being*, not for *doing*. God hates abuse. Abuse is not of God. Although He hates divorce, He does not hate the person who gets a divorce or is separated. "For the Lord, the God of Israel, says: I hate divorce and marital separation and him who covers his garment [his wife] with violence. Therefore keep a watch upon your spirit [that it may be controlled by My Spirit], that you deal not treacherously and faithlessly [with your marriage mate]" (Mal. 2:16, AMP.).

What does the Bible say about separation and divorce?

In Mal. 2:16 we read that God hates divorce, but He also says He hates the man who covers his wife with violence. Paul wrote in 1 Cor. 7:5, "Do not deprive one another except perhaps by agreement for a set time, to devote yourselves to prayer" (NRSV). If there is ever a time to separate with an

agreement and ever a time for prayer, it's in a domestic violence situation.

Life Skills has developed a structured separation flow chart
that we have used successfully for years. It contains directives
for each spouse and a time frame to give each space for
growth, maturing, and the resolution of individual issues and
conflicts. The agreement is then signed and the directives put
into place.

The Bible tells us not to divorce except in the case of
adultery. Let us look at what adultery really is. Rom. 2:22 says,
"You who say not to commit adultery, do you commit adultery
[are you unchaste in action or in thought]?" (AMP.). Adultery
can be physical, emotional, or fantasy in the theater of the
mind. Jesus said, "Everyone who so much as looks upon a
woman with evil desire for her has already committed adultery with her in his heart" (Matt. 5:28, AMP). Many times the
Church looks at the physical as the only way to commit adultery. When you give more affection to someone else than you
do your spouse, or a friendship with the opposite sex is better
than with your spouse, then you have put yourself into a dangerous situation that can lead to an emotional affair. Then in
time it can and may lead to a physical affair.

Physical affairs start with a fantasy. The mind can visualize
and animate a still picture or a visual fantasy. Thus, it can
carry on a sordid animated thought pattern with supposedly
no consequences. Fantasy is the act of putting a face to the
pornography in your mind from the things you've seen, experienced, or desired. After five to seven times of fantasizing
about a situation or a person, the mind starts to believe it as
reality. This is especially dangerous when the person has used
the fantasy for self-gratification. The mind sees the animated
picture, and the physical body responds. The message to the
mind is "This is an actual relationship" and the reactive behavior is to let down the barrier in reality and pursue what
the mind perceives as an "already done deal."

What does God think about abuse?

God hates abuse. Exod. 22:22 says, "Do not take advantage of a widow or an orphan." Jesus said in Luke 4:18, "He has anointed me to preach good news to the poor. He has sent me to proclaim freedom for the prisoners and recovery of sight for the blind, to release the oppressed." Again, Mal. 2:16 says clearly, "For the Lord, the God of Israel, says: I hate divorce and marital separation and him who covers his garment [his wife] with violence" (AMP.). Ps. 72:14 reads, "He will redeem their lives from oppression and fraud and violence, and precious and costly shall their blood be in His sight" (AMP.).

What does submission have to do with all of this?

Many times in the Church world submission is held over the heads of women by men who are emotionally manipulative or abusive in order to get their way and maintain power and control. Scriptural submission is just as great for the husband as it is for the wife.

Eph. 5:25-28 reminds us that as Christ died for the Church, a man should give his life for his wife. A childish, abusive man will spiritually abuse his wife by telling her that she has to be subjected to her husband in everything. He does not realize that a husband's mandate is to literally be willing to sacrifice his life for her. Which is the greater submission? The greater submission is for the man. 1 Pet. 3:5-6 in essence says that the wife should not be terrified, fearful, or full of anxiety in a godly home. The passage as a whole speaks to the man with a mandate of creating a very safe place where she is not terrified or living in fear and anxiety. Let us look at the rest of the mandate.

1 Pet. 3:7-9 goes on to give the pattern for husbandry when it states that a husband should live as follows: considerately, intelligently recognizing the marriage relationship, honoring the woman as physically weaker, recognizing the equality (joint heirs of grace), one in the same mind (united in spirit), sympathizing with his wife, loving his wife, compassionately, courteously, tenderheartedly, humble-mindedly,

never returning evil for evil, never returning insult for insult, never scolding, never given to tongue-lashing, never berating, always blessing, praying for his wife's welfare and happiness, praying for his wife's protection, truly pitying (empathizing), truly loving.

If a husband will follow this pattern, the family will be blessed as a unit. If a man rebels against these principles, his prayers will be hindered and cut off, and he will not be able to pray effectively (1 Pet. 3:7).

From this research in God's Word, it is the author's conclusion that the only prayer that God hears from a man who abuses his wife and family is the prayer of repentance. All other requests are hindered or denied because of God's hatred of violence.

What should I expect of my friends, my pastor, my counselor?

It is a sad state of affairs in the church that when a woman has been abused, it seems that the congregation, her friends, and her clergy shy away from dealing with the situation. Friends don't know what to say and are afraid to hear what the victim is really saying, so she feels forsaken by those she should be able to lean on the most.

Let's describe what a true friend is before we go on. This is a person to whom you can tell your confidential information without the fear of betrayal unless it is life-threatening. This is called trust.

How can you as a friend help an abused woman?

- Listen and believe. Be ready to listen to what she has to say and for as long as it takes her to say it.
- Demonstrate genuine concern. The victim needs to know you care about her as an individual and that you are truly her friend.
- Be trustworthy and calm. The victim needs to know she can open up to you and that it is safe to do so.
- Be patient. Do not expect her to move quickly through the process of change. If she is in immediate danger, you may want to invite her and her children

to stay in your home for a night or two until you or someone can help her find another safe place.

- Educate yourself. Know the available services in your area and the procedures to follow in calling law enforcement or an agency. Get acquainted with the shelters and services for battered women in your area.
- Encourage the victim. Help her to understand that she does have choices, and allow her to make her own choices. Be careful not to encourage her to stay in an abusive situation. This can be life threatening. Remind her that she isn't crazy.
- Help her to realize that she's not responsible for her husband's violent behavior.
- Remind her that God does not want her to suffer abuse. He wants her to be treated with love and respect.
- Help her to see herself as capable and lovable.
- Be alert to signs of abuse. These could include long sleeves in the summer, sunglasses indoors, withdrawal from social occasions, as well as unexplained or feeble excuses for her injuries.
- Reassure the children and help where you can in meeting their needs.
- Pray with her and for her.

What not to do

- Do not tell her to stay in the violent home.
- Do not lose patience, be judgmental, or give advice.
- Do not tell her she's insane for staying in a situation.
- Do not tell her that you wouldn't put up with such treatment.
- Do not try to talk to her husband or confront him yourself.
- Do not try to intervene in a violent episode; instead call the police.

Many pastors are afraid to look at or get involved with the situation, because "this does not happen in my church." During one of our trainings at Life Skills, one of the pastors in the group stood up and stated emphatically that he had been a pastor for 23 years in various cities and had never had to deal one time with emotional or physical abuse. His consensus was that we were making a mountain out of a molehill, exaggerating the problem, making something out of nothing. Emotional and physical abuse does not exist in the Body of Christ, he said. Needless to say, this seems to be the mindset of many churches and denominations. Statistics tell us that abuse within the church is as great, if not greater, than that in the secular world. Thus, there is often no safe place, even in the church, for an abused woman to find help or hope.

Judy. I am reminded of my own experience when I was abused for so long, then separated and divorced. I turned to the church for friendship and for someone to listen but found no one—including the pastor, who had no time for me. I got a quick prayer and a pat on the hand from another pastor, as if I had a contagious disease and he was afraid he would contract it. Another pastor just couldn't find time in his schedule to talk to me. I have discovered that they're afraid of the single or abused woman, so therefore they shun them all. They refuse to believe that the husband could be as she describes—after all, he may be a member of the choir, a church leader, a Sunday School teacher, or even a close friend. We have even seen pastors who have issues of abuse. This book will cover more of what to expect from a pastor later.

Many counselors do not have the background or knowledge to understand the dynamics of domestic violence. When looking for a counselor, ask questions such as "Do you have any experience in working with family violence?" Check his or her background and training. Don't be afraid to ask the counselor specific questions: "Do you do couple counseling with violent families?" If the answer is yes, he or she is not qualified to deal with the issues of victimization. The number-one rule in working with violent families is individual counseling.

My husband hasn't hit me, and yet I know something's wrong. Could I be abused?

There are 20 areas of abuse, and only one is physical (see Figure 1, chapter 2). If you live in fear or feel unsafe, something is definitely wrong. There is the possibility of emotional abuse of some kind. Be safe—develop a safety plan.

How can I persuade my husband to get help?

You can't. Get help for yourself. As you develop your personality, develop your individuality, set goals and boundaries, and in essence get a life, he'll start feeling left out and will start reacting as he loses control. If there is physical abuse in the home, then consequences are the only thing the partner will understand. This may mean a structured separation under the supervision of a trained counselor. Most of the time the abuser is motivated by loss and the fear of abandonment.

Should we consider counseling as a couple?

Definitely not! The abuser has a dual personality that he has perfected over the years to hide the dark side. To the outside world he looks good and knows the right words. He has developed a survival technique and can con a counselor or pastor who is not aware of the dynamics.

The typical scenario of couples counseling in which the spouse is abusive looks like this: They go to the first session and try to get acquainted. He is outgoing, somewhat talkative or maybe too talkative, blaming and explaining her problems. He may even hide behind religious terminology and scripture. If the counselor asks her if there is any emotional, sexual, or physical abuse, she will not be able to disclose the truth in front of the spouse, fearing what will happen when they leave the session. Thus, her trust has been betrayed and the counselor has lost all credibility in her mind. She shuts down and loses hope. After two or three sessions, the counselor generally focuses on her problems, her depression, and very possibly her need for medication. Many times the husband convinces the counselor that he doesn't need further counseling. One more time he has manipulated her to believe she's crazy.

At Life Skills, the procedure is to counsel the woman in a safe place without her spouse present. You'll need to build trust so that she'll know she will not be betrayed and that she'll be believed. She may tell the story over and over again because nobody has ever listened to her. This gives the counselor the insight to the abuse that the spouse is perpetrating. The counselor then counsels the spouse individually. Having the knowledge of the dynamics in the home, the counselor is able to direct the questioning of the spouse for accountability and responsibility. If there is emotional and physical abuse, Life Skills recommends nine months to one year of individual counseling before bringing the couple together.

My husband hit me once. Will it happen again?

Most likely if he has hit once, he will hit again. The longer we are in relationships without resolving our conflicts, the more we escalate in our anger and our need to control. It is like being on an addictive drug, always needing more. It may start out as verbal, then hitting walls or tables, which creates fear. Finally tables, walls, and screaming are not enough. You never really know when he will choose you as the next object of his anger and abuse.

We have seen couples who have had verbal and emotional abuse in their relationship for 25 to 30 years, and then the abuse becomes physical. Many at that point come for help when they should have come years before to deal with the core issues that lead to the physical incident.

My husband says if I hadn't provoked him, he wouldn't have lost control. Is this true?

This is not true. No behavior of any woman justifies or provokes violence. No woman ever deserves to be hit, shoved, kicked, or physically hurt in any way. A woman does not provoke her husband. She should have the right of expression, the right to express feelings and opinions. She has the right to express anxieties, fears, and thoughts. She has the right to be involved in the decision-making process in their relationship. She has a right to ask questions and get a civil response. She has a right to disagree and to resolve conflicts without his seeing her as the enemy. She has the right to feel safe in her home. Here is the problem—a controlling man has no ability to recognize that she is a partner and that they are to be a team. He sees her as a possession instead of an individual of value, thus becoming a threat to his pattern of control. He sees all of her rights as a person as provocation and defiance of his authority. He is responsible for his reactive behavior. He should be in control of his anger, which may mean taking a "time out" or seeking counseling.

Why do I feel like a child in this relationship?

The man who is controlling in a relationship takes on the power not only of the husband but also of the father. She is a possession to him, and he feels he has the right to mold her, guide her, clone her for his selfish wants, and then feels he has a right to punish her for rebelling or not complying to his demands. A true healthy relationship approaches every issue on an adult-to-adult level—communication, conflict resolution, personal growth, maturity, and bonding. In the unhealthy relationship, one takes the power of a parent and pushes the partner into a child mode. To heal, the one who feels like a child needs a support system to help understand how to move to the adult level and to develop individuality and identity. This is a process that takes time. Be patient with yourself.

I feel as if everything that goes wrong is my fault.

Men who are controlling have never developed their core personalities nor their identities. They live in a shame base, which says, "I am my behavior." In their minds, to question their behavior is to question them as persons. This creates a childish type of adult who can never be wrong. They learn at a very early age to blame someone, a circumstance, or a situation so that they do not have to be accountable or responsible for their reactions, decisions, or behavior. By the time such a man is in a relationship, he has perfected his survival techniques to the point that it is always the fault of the spouse, the children, the boss, the pastor, and so on. If something is successful, he grabs the glory; if it goes wrong, it's somebody else's fault. This is a person who is also opinionated and will fight to convince others that his opinion is right.

Why was he so wonderful when we dated?

The old saying "She dated the man and married the boy" holds true. A man who is controlling has developed a dual personality, one for the outside world, which is not consistent or stable, and one that he reverts back to behind closed doors. This is called a Jekyll-and-Hyde personality. Until he is sure of the commitment or affection, he exhibits only the caring, outgoing, kind, generous, mannerly, nice guy. This is part of his conquest. The change comes when he is able to have sex and possess her or he marries her, creating ownership. He has conquered the prize and now, because of the physical intimacy that he has achieved, he lowers the barriers and starts his control methods to show who is king of the castle. Now she sees the other side, because he cannot maintain the mask of a good side 24 hours a day.

Do I have to stay with him for the sake of the children?

The safety of a child is that Dad loves Mom, and Mom loves Dad. This creates a safe, supportive, nurturing environment in which to grow up. We have seen over the years as we have talked with children and watched their behavior that they display the dysfunctions of the home. A son who grows up seeing violence or abuse in the home will more likely than not become an abuser and perpetrate this into the next generation. A girl who grows up in this type of dysfunction will become a victim just like her mother most of the time.

Judy. I was a victim myself, but after the divorce the kids got angry with me. I later came to find out that they were angrier with me than with Paul because they couldn't understand why I hadn't left years earlier and why I allowed him to treat us so badly. Their home was never safe. To this day they still struggle with the anxiety created in those years by the uncertainty of when he would get angry again and what he might do the next time.

Should I give him another chance?

When there has been an abusive incident, there needs to be a consequence. As with a child who acts out, wrong behavior needs to be followed by a consequence. Men who are abusive generally were raised in homes in which there were threats, warnings, and possible abuse, but not a direct consequence for their behavior. They learn to talk themselves out of situations and learn to blame others, situations, or circumstances. We believe that a man can change, but it takes time and a third-party intervention. He cannot do it alone. He will promise anything, even church counseling, but has no capability without learning, knowledge, discipline, accountability, and responsibility. These things are learned; they do not come naturally. The victim has been hurt, trust has been broken, and most of the time hope has been lost. Only after he has received help and has proven his change over a period of time—which may include some testing on your part due to the lack of trust—should you even begin any process toward reconciliation. Remember that old saying "Actions speak louder than words." We all need to know that the change is for real this time instead of the words mouthed. Anyone can promise anything. Reconciliation is a process and takes time. It took time to get into this situation, and it's going to take time to change it.

I've been told I need to set boundaries. What does that mean? How do I set a boundary?

The victim in this type of situation has generally come from a home where there were no boundaries. To tell someone to set boundaries creates fear. To learn to do so takes a support system to help understand the dynamics of the dysfunctional home and to help us see what normal is. This is part of the process of growing up, learning conflict resolution, communications, anger management, and developing identity.

By understanding what normal is and developing an identity, I then identify my victimization and learn to say no. A boundary says, "I will not allow you to do that to me again; there will be a consequence." Establish what the consequence will be, and then hold your ground. The consequence may be calling the police, a structured separation, intense counseling, and so on.

One couple we worked with told us their story concerning consequences. The day they married she warned him that if he ever hit her he should never go to sleep, because she would get even. Three weeks later he hit her. She waited over two weeks and didn't respond. He thought she had forgotten all about it. He was taking a nap, sound asleep and only in his underwear, when she came into the room and saw him asleep. She went to the garage, picked up a four-foot-long board, went back to the bedroom, and whacked him with all her strength across the back of his thighs. He jumped up yelling and screaming. Her response was that there would be no second chance. "Don't you ever hit me again," she said. He got the message, and for 25 years they lived with no physical violence, yet sad to say, a lot of emotional abuse went on in those 25 years. The moral of the story? Set boundaries.

QUESTIONS FROM THE MAN WHO ABUSES

Why am I out of control?

As you studied in an earlier chapter, if you were wounded before the age of accountability and your developmental process has been frozen, you are locked into the age of directives and become very dependent, making you unable to make decisions. You can make decisions for other people and control their lives, but decisions for your life are made by indecision, circumstances, situations, and other people. You have no control of your life, so you try to manipulate and control circumstances, situations, and other people. This produces a life of chaos.

I hate what I do, so why do I do it?

When you are wounded in early childhood, you never reach the age of decision emotionally. Many times you know what you should do, but you are driven by your irrational belief systems and survival methods to maintain control. You end up doing what you hate because you are driven by your wounds and unresolved conflicts. You end up acting like an undisciplined child, doing what you want to do instead of doing what you know you should do. Although you know right from wrong, you still live an undisciplined life.

I only restrain her. Is that physical abuse?

Yes. Earlier in this book we looked at the various areas of abuse, and restraining is one of the areas considered as physical abuse and is against the law. Many times when a man is restraining his partner he has escalated in his anger and does not sense his own strength. We have seen cases in which women have been restrained, and on the inside of their upper arms are fingerprint-size bruises left by his "just restraining" her so she couldn't hit him back.

My home is my "castle." Why can't she just do as I say?

This is medieval thinking. The Scriptures have always told us that we are one as we come together in a marriage relationship. The marriage contract creates a new entity called "we." A true marriage relationship is a partnership and a team effort. Her input and opinion to any given situation should be valued and encouraged, because she adds a different perspective, which creates a broader view toward making decisions and seeing the reality of the situation (Eph. 5:28-30).

Sometimes I love her; sometimes I hate her. Why?

If your wounds of childhood have stopped your developmental process, you have never developed your core or real personality and character. You then develop a pseudopersonality that is not a true identity. This personality consists of the expectations of important people in your life from whom you fear rejection. The pseudopersonality then becomes very changeable, depending on who you're with and where you are. "A double minded man is unstable in all his ways" (James 1:8, KJV). This is the foundation of the Jekyll-and-Hyde personality that we referred to earlier. Our love-hate relationships with parents, siblings, spouse, children, and friends are based on the lack of core personality development, maturity, and character. As you grow and mature, you then become single-minded, putting away childish things and childish thinking (1 Cor. 13:11). You then are in control of your decisions and your own life. Love is a choice based on maturity and commitment.

If she would get help, we would be OK—wouldn't we?

Again this question goes back to developmental fixation. If you are stuck in the age of directives, the stage where parents fix everything, then you are always looking for a mommy to make it right for you because you cannot resolve your own conflicts. You grow chronologically, marry, and many times you make a mommy out of your spouse. When you are in crisis, you try to get her to fix it, or in essence if she'll get help, then everything will be OK. This becomes your way of escaping your own responsibilities and blame-shifting the responsibility to her. This never resolves the core problem because this is an individual issue, not a marriage issue. You are the one to get help through counseling.

Why doesn't she love me the way I think she should?

Most men see their role of love in a marriage relationship as performance or sex. Performance, to a man, means, "I pay the rent, I buy the groceries, I furnish the house," and so on. Sex means, "She takes care of my physical needs, cleans the house, takes care of the kids in return for my performance." This is not necessarily a man's conscious thought process but more of a subtle assumption driven by society, learned behavior, and wounds of childhood. No one has ever taught us what "real" love, intimacy, and bonding are. The Scriptures tell us that we should learn these things from the elders. But in our society the family has been so wounded and torn apart that we grow up trying to reinvent what we think is love.

Why doesn't she want to make love anymore?

There are distinct emotional differences between male and female. Sexuality to the male is a physical event. It can be focused on and played out in a very short time. A man can detach from conflict, outside distractions, commitments, communication, and so on and have sex for the sake of sex or self-gratification. To a woman, sex is part of her whole life, her very being. In her mind it is a much bigger picture. This picture includes trust, commitment, bonding, intimacy, responsibility, accountability, communication, promises kept, respect, tenderness, and concern for her and the children. When a man abuses his spouse, he gives her the message that she is good for only one thing—sex. When she gets this message, she shuts down sexually, and then he has to start the wooing process all over again.

Her sexual response in a marriage begins in the dating stage by developing an intimate, nonsexual friendship, which develops a foundation of trust. As the courting process continues, he develops his nonsexual intimacy, that is, getting to know her, hearing about her childhood experiences, getting to know about her family background. He gives her respect, and love builds, creating a validation that lets her know that she is loved for who she is, not for what she does. A nonsexual courtship to the marriage altar establishes her honor and validates her identity. At Life Skills we have an exercise for married couples that involves beginning a nonsexual dating process to reestablish the wife's honor and value.

Shouldn't she be the one to leave?

This ties in to the "king of the castle" question we covered earlier. In the last 25 years of the domestic violence movement it has usually been the woman who has had to leave the home. Again, this is medieval thinking. The man who controls the family also controls the finances and then expects the woman to leave and make it on her own. He has abused, intimidated, controlled, and hurt her, yet she has to take the children, disrupt their lives, and flee from the home to a shelter. She then experiences very little privacy and very little, if any, financial benefits. Generally she is in the shelter for one to three weeks and returns to a home where every dish has been used, the trash is piled up, the laundry has not been done, and he is angry, demanding that she perform her duties around the house, including having sex. We feel that since the man has more access to resources and that the children are the other innocent victims, he should be the one to leave the home and leave the wife and children in their familiar surroundings and continue financial support.

If she is going to act like a child, shouldn't I treat her like one?

A marriage consists of two adults who may be wounded and many times have a tendency to respond childishly. That does not give the spouse the right to move to the parent role and punish or treat the partner like a child. If one is hurting, the other should support and encourage during that time. If this happens often, then counseling should be considered. The mind recognizes actions more than verbalization. If a man treats his wife like a child, her sexual drive for him will diminish very quickly. Our minds are programmed not to have sex with a parent. A husband acts like a rigid disciplinarian parent, and she shuts down. Again, actions speak louder than words.

After all I have done for her, how can she do this to me?

Too many marriages are based on "I'll do for you if you do for me." This is self-centered, childish thinking. A child is motivated only by reward or "what's in it for me." An adult is supposed to see the greater picture, which is the long-term bonding process, which builds relationships and intimacy.

Abuse shatters this bond. Unconditional love is giving of yourself, expecting nothing in return (1 Cor. 13).

Why does she always act like my mother?

The model the parents exhibit in front of their children sets the expectation of the children for their own marriages. Whether we like it or not, men have the tendency to marry women like their moms. They may have had ambivalent (love-hate) relationship with their mothers, but they learned to cope. They then date, and many times think they've chosen dating partners not like their mothers. They may think they have picked someone completely the opposite of their parent, but there are underlying familiarities they are not aware of. Subconsciously it is familiar territory, making it easier to cope. We do have an ability to cope with what is familiar to us, because it's comfortable and doesn't require new thinking. If we are arrested in development, we will subconsciously put our spouse in a mothering role, including calling her "Mother," to take care of us, then resent the fact that she is doing what we have forced her to do.

I didn't hurt her that badly. Why is she overreacting? I said I'm sorry—isn't that good enough?

Many times an abusive spouse feels his wife is overreacting because he doesn't want to be accountable for his responses and his behaviors. Very seldom when a man has created the wound does he want to listen to her, take responsibility, and live with the consequences of his behavior. A woman generally does not overreact to the first offense. In the beginning the man will say he is sorry, and she wants to believe him. As time goes on and the events continue to escalate, the "I'm sorry" comes to mean nothing. After some time he uses "I'm sorry" as a manipulative tool to keep her off his back. "I'm sorry" begins to mean "I said I'm sorry—what do you want me to do, bleed for you, lie down and die, or what? You're supposed to forgive me and go on with life. After all, doesn't it say in the Bible to forgive and forget?" This is nothing more than spiritual abuse and an excuse to avoid responsibility and consequences for his actions. The consequences that he wants to avoid are her feelings and the resolution of the issue at hand. He now has shifted the responsibility of his actions over to her for not forgiving and not responding. Many times after a cycle of violence, escalation, abuse, and the honeymoon stage, he wants sex and wants it immediately. This is not love or restoration; it's only conquest and another form of abuse. He knows that to abuse is to break the marriage covenant (Eph. 5:28-30). Family violence is breaking the law. It is a crime.

I'm afraid I might hurt her really badly. Could I?

Anytime we do not deal with our anger and emotions we have the potential to lash out emotionally and physically. Much of our anger and rage goes back to childhood, and those issues that have never been resolved keep festering. As we grow older, we stack on top of that festering wound new unresolved issues. After awhile, anger becomes our second nature. We trigger easily, react without thinking, and set a course toward destruction. This is the foundation for lashing out and badly hurting the ones we love. Songs have been written about this syndrome, stressing the observation that we hurt only those we love. To even think of this question of possibly hurting one's wife means we need help. Let's take the first step.

This was a personal problem. Why did she call the police?

She was afraid. She wonders if this will be the time when she may be permanently injured or killed. A living being—man, woman, or child—was never created to be abused. The Bible is very clear on the issue of violence (see Ps. 55). Domestic violence is a crime. When a person has been abused, a crime has been committed, and intervention is a proper procedure. Too many "personal problems" cost the lives of women who guarded the secret. Abuse deserves a consequence. Most men who are abusive do not acknowledge that they are responsible for their behavior.

Why can't she keep her mouth shut?

This is a protection of the abuser's dual personality. He thinks he has everyone else conned, that nobody else suspects that he could do such a thing. If she tells, it may ruin his reputation, job, ministry, social standing, friendships, relationship to his parents, and so on. Many times the victim will share with a friend what is happening, and the friend will not believe her because he or she has never seen that side of the abuser's personality. She begins to isolate herself and thinks something's wrong with her. The abuse continues until she can't take it anymore, so she takes a chance and speaks out; the abuser then feels betrayed. She should have asked for help earlier. She has no obligation to keep the secret any longer and keep the abuse going.

WHAT CAN MY CHURCH DO?

1. Be prepared to get involved.

Plan ahead. Do not get caught off guard. If the church is really committed to ministering to families, it must be prepared to provide the structural support. Consult with the professionals in your area to find out how to implement intervention with an abuser and how to provide protection for a victim and her children. Contact your local shelter.

2. Maintain follow-through.

Be persistent. It is easy to get discouraged when working with family violence. Progress is usually slow. Many times the abuser is in denial and does not want to change. Many times the victim is paralyzed by great fear. Expect the unexpected. Even setbacks can happen. Be faithful. It can be emotionally and physically draining, so don't allow just a few people to carry the load. An extensive prayer ministry is a must to support this outreach.

3. Establish a referral network for helping both the victim and the abuser.

A referral network should include housing, food, clothing, protective services, professional counseling, the criminal justice system, and employment referral services. Get acquainted, and use reputable agencies. The church should be a focal point for coordinating the network, but it should not be expected to do it all alone.

4. Hold the abuser accountable.

The church is responsible to show truth and mercy. If there has been a separation due to physical violence, regular accountability must be maintained. If charges have been filed and the male partner is in jail, he should not be abandoned. Indeed, he needs to know that what he has done is a crime and that God hates family violence. This is where the church can take a stand against spousal or partner abuse yet offer support with structure and accountability. This gives hope of healing for the abuser. Remember: he needs specialized counseling. Make this a part of your networking.

QUESTIONS FROM PASTORS AND COUNSELORS

What are the classic signs of an abusive man?

Lenore Walker in her book *The Battered Woman* has researched the common characteristics of a batterer. The abusive man exhibits many of the following characteristics:

1. Has low self-esteem.
2. Believes all the myths about battering relationships.
3. Is a traditionalist, believing in male supremacy.
4. Blames others for his actions.
5. Exhibits exaggerated jealousy. In order for him to feel secure, he must become overly involved in the woman's life. He is suspicious of her relationships with others.
6. Presents a dual personality.
7. Has severe stress reactions during which he uses drinking and wife-beating to cope.

8. Frequently uses sex as an aggressive act.

9. Does not believe his violent behavior should have negative consequences. Typically denies the problems; becomes enraged if woman reveals the true situation. Element of overkill/overdoing.

10. Batterers generally come from violent homes, or where a general lack of respect for women and children is evident. Relationships with mothers were often ambivalent [love/hate].

11. Personality distortion is frequent. Social loner or involved only superficially. Extremely sensitive to differences in others' behavior.

12. Is found in all socioeconomic levels, all educational, racial, and age-groups.

13. Exhibits poor impulse control, explosive temper, and limited tolerance of frustration.

14. Has insatiable ego needs [a quality of childlike narcissism not generally detectable to people outside family group].

15. Exhibits qualities that suggest great potential for change and improvement, that is, frequent "promises" for the future.

16. Believes he has poor social skills; describes relationship with his mate as the closest he has ever known; remains in contact with family.[1]

Some questions to ask about someone you suspect may be an abuser:

1. Did he grow up in a violent family?

2. Does he tend to use force or violence to "solve" his problems?

3. Does he abuse alcohol or other drugs?

4. Does he think poorly of himself?

5. Does he have strong traditional ideas about what a man should be and what a woman's role should be?

6. Is he jealous of other men in her life, of her girlfriends, her family, or her job?

7. Does he "keep tabs" on her?

8. Does he want to know where she is at all times?

Why can't I do couples counseling?

The victim and the abuser should always be counseled separately to deal with individual issues that were existing before either came together. Research has shown that over 90 percent of the issues a couple needs to deal with are rooted before the age of puberty. In couples counseling the victim does not have the freedom to talk about the abuse in the relationship. This also places the victim at risk for retaliation in the form of severe abuse, which creates a lethal factor. Counselors need to be aware that the abuser will virtually always deny the abuse. Out of shame and fear, the battered woman will be reluctant to talk about the violence. Remember: safety first, counseling second.

Whom do I believe?

The structure of counseling for the abusive family is to bring the woman in separately and interview her before interviewing the husband. As stated before, if a woman feels she is safe with her counselor and is sure she won't be betrayed, she will be truthful about the abuse within the family unit. Over 80 percent of women who reach out for help for the first time go to clergy or a Christian counselor. Many times the abused woman has tried to share her pain and has not been believed, so she goes back into isolation and feels there is no hope. Listen carefully; let her express herself, and believe her.

When do I need to separate them?

Ask if there is physical violence. "Does he hit you?" "Are you in danger?" "How does he express his temper?" Always try to separate them if you find that there is physical violence. Many times the emotional abuse is so great that there needs to be a separation, but this has to be dealt with case by case. Very seldom will the court systems recognize or prosecute emotional abuse charges, as they are hard to prove. Bruises can be photographed, but emotional abuse cannot be seen with the eye. To a trained counselor the body language displays the emotional abuse. Emotional abuse hurts worse and can last a lifetime. Life Skills has developed a structured separation flow chart that gives the counselor and the clients direction for the separation.

"The prudent see danger and take refuge" (Prov. 27:12).

How do I tap the resources in my community?

Shelters: Call the victim/witness program in your local court system and express your desire to be educated and get acquainted with the resources in the community. Many times a shelter number is not published, but the court system, law enforcement personnel, or State Coalition against Domestic Violence can give you numbers for the shelters. Call the shelter director and explain who you are. Tell her that you're wanting to get involved in the community and want to be part of the solution to this problem. As a counselor or pastor, never show up at a shelter without calling first. They do have strict policies for the safety and confidentiality of their clients. Offer a church room to the shelter for community support groups free of charge and offer baby-sitting. Coordinate a church response team who can provide rides to doctor appointments, court dates, and so on. Perhaps the team can solicit donations for deposits on utilities or apartments for the victim and offer baby-sitting for her children.

Legal Aid Services: Find out what legal services are available. Are there attorneys who will do pro bono work for women who are in crisis? Find out which lawyers are informed about the issues of wife assault.

Hospitals and Emergency Rooms: Doctors and nurses do have a network to support the battered woman and to serve her and get her to safety. They also will welcome a pastor/counselor who will take interest in procedures, victim support, and safety.

Law Enforcement Personnel: A pastor/counselor should meet and work with law enforcement personnel. Find out the law enforcement policies such as whether the arrest is made at the officer's discretion; the no-drop policy; jail time; and so

on. Most agencies now have a domestic violence department.
They also welcome those who want to learn about the problem and may allow a pastor to ride along on a shift and be involved with domestic violence calls, especially if the pastor
has any training in the domestic violence area. A woman
from the church may volunteer as an advocate in the courts
or shelter systems.

Court Systems: The pastor or staff should connect with
prosecutors, probation officers, judges, and victim/witness
programs, acquainting themselves with how the courts are
structured. Advocate programs are a good entry level for pastors to start their networking. Advocates can also help get
temporary restraining orders, no contact orders, or full restraining orders. This knowledge will be a great help in secur-
ing safety for the victim.

Batterers' Treatment/Counseling Programs: Look for a Family Life Skills group in your city or region. Check out men's
treatment programs and get acquainted with the directors.

What is my role/responsibility as a pastor toward the victim?

A pastor needs understanding before he or she gets involved with the victim. Listen empathetically. Help the woman and children find safety and support.

What about submission?

Let me share this scenario. A woman who is a member of
the church has been in an abusive relationship for years. She
confronts her husband and tells him that she's going to talk to
the pastor about the abuse. The husband threatens her and
curses the pastor, yet she goes to the counseling appointment
anyway. As she shares her heart with the pastor, the pastor
wonders what she does to cause her husband to act like this.
She feels as though she is to blame for her own abuse as the
pastor continues to talk to her about submission. If she would
cook better meals, keep a cleaner house, be more attractive,
be more seductive, pray harder, and try to meet his needs,
maybe the abuse would stop. She goes home feeling defeated

and hopeless. This is dangerous and puts the woman and children at great risk. As she walks through the door the husband screams, "What did that [expletive] pastor have to say?" She tells her husband that the pastor told her to cook better meals, keep a cleaner house, be more attractive, be more seductive, and try to meet his needs—then maybe the abuse would stop. The husband responds with excitement that the pastor is on his side. He's even thinking about maybe going to church and possibly becoming friends with the pastor. Once again she has been victimized by spiritual phrases and terminology. As we shared earlier, submission is for both, on an equal basis according to Eph. 5:22, 28-30.

If we cannot find trust in the church with supposedly godly people, then how can we possibly find trust in God for healing of these problems? Most of the time the victim feels so alone in a church filled with people. Please reach out and believe her, along with making her feel welcome and that God cares, and so do you. Do not make her responsible for the problem.

But he's a deacon, board member, Sunday School teacher—it's me.

Men who are abusive come from all walks of life, all nationalities, all socioeconomic levels, and all religious groups. They know no boundaries relative to class, income, or background. It is very disturbing to realize that violence is part of life of many faithful churchgoing families. This is one problem the church should be addressing, but it's probably the problem that we ignore the most. "My people are destroyed from lack of knowledge," Hos. 4:6 reads. It has been the passion of Life Skills International to educate the Body of Christ to deal with this issue rather than sweep it under the carpet or pretend "It doesn't exist in our congregation." There is hope and help for hurting families, but as Jer. 6:14 says, "You can't heal a wound by saying it's not there!" (TLB).

It's time that we in the Body of Christ recognize our problems, that we become accountable and mature. It is also proper to address these issues from the pulpit. When a pastor understands the issues that others face, then those in the congregation who are hurting will respond.

NOTES

Chapter 2

1. Lonni Collins Pratt, "God, Go Away," *Herald of Holiness*, August 1992, 26.

2. Televised news conference from the White House, Washington, D.C., CBS television network, March 1, 1989.

3. Murray A. Straus, Richard J. Gelles, and Suzanne K. Steinmetz. *Behind Closed Doors: Violence in the American Family* (New York: Anchor Press, 1981).

4. Statistics from the United States Federal Bureau of Investigation Report on Domestic Violence, Net Benefits "Cause of the Month," Internet site at <www.netbenefits.com/causes/html>.

5. Surgeon General, United States Public Health Services, *Journal of the American Medical Association* 276, no. 23 (June 17, 1992), 3132.

6. NBC Nightly News, NBC television network, October 1996. Also, "Domestic Violence," on the television series *The Justice Files*, Discovery Channel, 1998. Also, "The Facts," Family Violence Prevention Fund, Internet site, 1998.

7. "Fact Sheet," Colorado Coalition Against Domestic Violence, Internet site at<www.psynet.net/ccav>, 1998.

8. R. A. Berk et al., "The Dark Side of Families," paper on family violence research (Beverly Hills, Calif.: Sage, 1983).

9. "Fact Sheet," Colorado Coalition Against Domestic Violence, Internet site at<www.psynet.net/ccav>, 1998.

10. P. Claus and M. Ranel, "Special Report: Family Violence," United States Bureau of Justice Statistics, undated.

11. Elizabeth Schneider, "Legal Reform Efforts for Battered Women," report (self-published, 1990).

12. "Fact Sheet," Colorado Coalition Against Domestic Violence, Internet site at<www.psynet.net/ccav>, 1998.

13. "Forgotten Victims of Family Violence," *Social Work*, July 1982.

14. "Fact Sheet," Colorado Coalition Against Domestic Violence, Internet site at<www.psynet.net/ccav>, 1998.

15. Straus et al., *Behind Closed Doors*.

16. Lucy Friedman and Sara Cooper, "The Cost of Domestic Violence," report from Victim Services Research Department, New York, 1987.

17. "Domestic Violence for Health Care Providers," report (Denver: Colorado Coalition Against Domestic Violence, 1991).

18. "Five Issues in American Health," report, American Medical Association, 1991.

Chapter 4

1. Berk et al., "The Dark Side of Families."
2. Adapted from L. E. Walker, *The Battered Woman* (New York: Harper and Row, 1979), 35-37. Used by permission.
3. Ibid., 31-33. Used by permission.
4. Adapted from V. Boyd and K. Klingbeil, "Behavioral Characteristics of Domestic Violence," report, n.p., 1979. Also Ruth S. Kempe and C. Henry Kempe, *The Abused Child* (Cambridge, Mass.: Harvard University Press, 1978), 26-42. Also Kendall Johnson, "Children's Reactions to Trauma," *Trauma in the Lives of Children* (Claremont, Calif.: Hunter House Publishers, 1989), 33-61.
5. Quoted in Karen Burton Mains, *Abuse in the Family* (Elgin, Ill.: David C. Cook Publishing Co., 1987), 7-8.

Chapter 5

1. Personal interviews with Elden M. Chalmers, Bismarck, N.Dak., February 1993.

Chapter 8

1. "Battle of the Sexes," videotaped program moderated by Scott Ross, produced by *The 700 Club*, television program of the Christian Broadcasting Network, Virginia Beach, Virginia, July 19, 1991.

For Reflection

1. Walker, *The Battered Woman*, 35-37. Used by permission.

BIBLIOGRAPHY

In addition to those listed in the Notes, the following works were used in the research and compiling of the indicated chapters.

Chapter 2

Ammermon, Robert T., and Michale Herson. *Assessment of Family Violence: A Clinical and Legal Sourcebook*. New York: John Wiley and Sons, 1992.

Cannon, Carol. *Never Good Enough*. Boise, Idaho: Pacific Press Publishing Assoc., 1993.

Hegstrom, Paul H. "Power and Control in Relationships." Case studies presented at three-day clinics in Denver. Self-published.

Russell, Diana E. H. *Rape in Marriage*. Bloomingdale, Ind., and Indianapolis: Indiana University Press, 1990.

Chapter 3

Amen, Daniel G., M.D. *Change Your Brain Change Your Life*. New York, Three Rivers Press, 1998.

Carter, Rita. *Mapping the Mind*. Los Angeles, University of California Press, 1999.

Harris, Maxine, Ph.D. *Trauma Recovery and Empowerment*. New York, The Free Press, 1998.

Hooper, Judith, and Dick Teresi, *The 3-Pound Universe*. New York, Macmillan Publishing Company, 1986.

Ornstein, Robert, and Richard F. Thompson, *The Amazing Brain*. Boston, Houghton Mifflin Company, 1984.

Williams, Tom, Psy.D. *Post Traumatic Stress Disorders*. Cincinnati, Ohio: Published by Disabled American Veterans, 1987.

Wilson, John P., Matthew J. Friedmon, and Jacob D. Lindy, Editors. *Treating Psychological Trauma & PTSD*. New York, The Guildford Press, 2001.

Van der Kolk, Bessel A., Alexander C. McFarlone, and Lars Weisaeth, Editors. *Traumatic Stress*. New York, The Guildford Press, 1996.

Personal interview with Marguerite McCormack, Supervisor of Columbine Connections, Denver, Colorado: 1999, 2001, 2003, video "Neurobiology of Trauma."

Chapter 4

Bijou, Sidney W., and Donald M. Baer. *Child Development: A Systematic and Empirical Theory*. New York: Appleton-Century-Crofts, 1961.

Bloom, Martin. *Life Span Development: Bases for Preventive and Interventive Helping*. New York: Macmillan Publishing Co., 1980.

Ells, Alfred. *Restoring Innocence*. Nashville: Thomas Nelson Publishers, 1990.

Erickson, Erik H. *Childhood and Society*. New York and London: W. W. Norton and Co., 1963.

————. *Identity and the Life Cycle*. New York and London: W. W. Norton and Co., 1980.

Garbarino, James, Edna Guttman, and Janis Wilson Seeley. *The Psychologically Battered Child*. San Francisco: Jossey-Bass Publishers, 1986.

Ginsburg, Herbert, and Sylvia Opper. *Piaget's Theory of Intellectual Development*. Englewood Cliffs, N.J.: Prentice-Hall, 1979.

Hagons, Kathryn B., and Joyce Case. *When Your Child Has Been Molested*. Lexington, Mass.: D. C. Heath Co., 1988.

Hofer, Myron A. *The Roots of Human Behavior*. San Francisco: W. H. Freeman and Co., 1981.

Kagon, Jerome. *Personality Development*. New York: Harcourt Brace Jovanovich, 1971.

Meiselman, Karin C. *Incest: A Psychological Study of Causes and Effects with Treatment Recommendations*. San Francisco: Jossey-Bass Publishers, 1984.

Piaget, Jean, and Barbel Inhelder. *The Psychology of the Child*. New York: Harper, 1969.

Spreen, Otfried, Anthony T. Risser, and Dorothy Edgell. *Developmental Neuropsychology*. New York: Oxford University Press, 1995.

Tobias, Cynthia Ulrich. *The Way They Learn*. Colorado Springs: Focus on the Family Publishers, 1994.

Wadsworth, Barry J. *Piaget's Theory of Cognitive Development*. New York, Longman, 1971.

Chapter 6

Albers, Robert H. *Shame: A Faith Perspective*. New York: Haworth Pastoral Press, 1995.

Eastman, Meg, and Sydney Croft Rozen. *Taming the Dragon in Your Child: Solutions for Breaking the Cycle of Family Anger*. New York: John Wiley and Sons, 1994.

Evans, Christine Brautigam. *Breaking Free of the Shame Trap*. New York: Ballantine Books, 1994.

Fossum, Merle A., and Marilyn J. Mason. *Facing Shame: Families in Recovery*. New York: W. W. Norton and Co., 1986.

Kaufman, Gershen. *Shame: The Power of Caring*. Rochester, Vt.: Schenkman Books, 1985.

Kurtz, Ernest. *Shame and Guilt: Characteristics of the Dependency Cycle*. Center City, Minn.: Hazelden Foundation, 1981.

LaHaye, Tim, and Bob Phillips. *Anger Is a Choice*. Grand Rapids: Zondervan, 1982.

Lester, Andrew D. *Coping with Your Anger: A Christian Guide*. Philadelphia: Westminster Press, 1983.

Lewis, Helen Block. *Shame and Guilt in Neurosis*. New York: International Universities Press, 1971.

Moore, James. *The Anger Kit*. Minneapolis: Self-published, 1981.

Moz, Jane Middleton. *Shame and Guilt: Masters of Disguise*. Deerfield Beach, Fla.: Health Communications, 1990.

Nathanson, Donald L. *Shame and Pride*. New York: W. W. Norton and Co., 1992.

Rubin, Theodore Isaac. *The Anger Book*. New York: Macmillan Publishing Co., 1993.

Smedes, Lewis B. *Shame and Grace*. New York: HarperCollins Publishers, 1993.

Tavris, Carol. *Anger: The Misunderstood Emotion*. New York: Simon and Schuster, 1989.

Warren, Neil Clark. *Make Anger Your Ally*. Garden City, N.Y.: Doubleday Publishers, 1985.

Wechsler, Harlan J. *What's So Bad About Guilt?* New York: Simon and Schuster, 1990.

West, Maxine. *Shame-Based Family Systems: The Assault on the Esteem*. Minneapolis: Self-published, 1986.

For Reflection

Bingham, Carol Findon. *Doorway to Response*. Springfield, Ill.: United Methodist Women Publishers, 1986.

Jackson, Tim, and Jeff Olson. *When Violence Comes Home: Help for Victims of Spouse Abuse*. Grand Rapids: Radio Bible Class, 1995.

Morris, Roberta. *Ending Violence in Families*. Toronto: United Church of Canada, 1988.

Rouse, Linda P. *You Are Not Alone: A Guide for Battered Women*. Holmes Beach, Fla.: Learning Publications, 1984.

Sutton, Cathy A., and Howard Green. *A Christian Response to Domestic Violence*. St. Davids, Pa.: NAACP in Social Work, 1985.

ABOUT THE AUTHOR

Paul Hegstrom lived the first 40 years of his life not understanding the driving force that caused him to self-destruct again and again. A failed marriage that was full of violence, a second relationship that was even more violent, $20,000 worth of therapy that could not bring change—and still the rage continued. Violence, drugs, and alcohol became a way of life until the threat of a long-term jail sentence brought him to the reality that he needed help. Facing severe consequences, Paul was motivated to discover the roots of his problems and begin the healing process.

The dramatic change of outlook in his life led Paul to take steps to help thousands of families facing the same jeopardy his suffered. Over 18,000 hours of research and 36,000 hours of facilitating domestic violence groups for women and developing a teen program were all a part of the development of the Life Skills program. In centers all around the world, the "Learning to Live, Learning to Love" program now brings help to hurting men, women, and children.

In addition, Paul remarried his first wife more than 20 years ago, and the second marriage has been free of emotional and physical abuse since its beginning. Paul and Judy Hegstrom live in Aurora, Colorado.

For more information on Life Skills International or any of its over 100 affiliate locations, offering seminars, workshops, training sessions, and personal appearances, interested readers are invited to contact the organization at any of the following addresses and numbers:

Life Skills International
P.O. Box 31227
Aurora, CO 80041

Life Skills International
651 Chambers Rd., Suite 200
Aurora, CO 80011
Telephone: 303-340-0598
Fax: 303-340-0052
E-mail: lsicorp@aol.com
Web site: www.lifeskillsintl.org